RESTORING THE BALANCE

Inspiring
Women

Restoring the BALANCE

Anne Le Tissier

CWR

Copyright © Anne Le Tissier, 2019

Published 2019 by CWR, Waverley Abbey House, Waverley Lane, Farnham, Surrey GU9 8EP, UK.

CWR is a Registered Charity – Number 294387 and a Limited Company registered in England – Registration Number 1990308.

The right of Anne Le Tissier to be identified as the author of this work has been asserted by her in accordance with the Copyright, Designs and Patents Act 1988.

For a list of National Distributors, visit cwr.org.uk/distributors

Scripture references are taken from the New International Version® Anglicised, NIV® Copyright © 1979, 1984, 2011 by Biblica, Inc.®

Other versions are marked: *The Message*, Copyright © 1993, 1994, 1995, 1996, 2000, 2001, 2002 by Eugene H. Peterson.

Concept development, editing, design and production by CWR.

Every effort has been made to ensure that this book contains the correct permissions and references, but if anything has been inadvertently overlooked the Publisher will be pleased to make the necessary arrangements at the first opportunity. Please contact the Publisher directly.

Cover image: Anika-Huizinga/Unsplash

Printed in the UK by Page Bros

ISBN: 978-1-78259-930-2

DEDICATION

For Mum – For her gentleness, care and love,
which informed and shaped my childhood and
teens; for her courage and devotion to God
through immense difficulties; and for walking
this journey of faith with me for the past
35 years. Thank You, Jesus, for letting me call
this wonderful woman 'Mum'.

Acknowledgements

Sincere thanks to Lynette Brooks, Director of Publishing and Ministry at CWR, for her interest in a conference I was teaching at Waverley Abbey House, which was the inspiration for this book. Thank you, Lynette, for your confidence in God's calling on my life, but also for your support when I reached out to you for prayer. Thanks also to Rebecca Berry, Lead Editor, for her patience with my questions and her most helpful replies. And of course to Andrea Bodle, for her thorough command of the manuscript and insightful editing expertise; as always, the CWR editing and publishing team excel in creativity, inspiration and skill – I so love working with you guys.

My husband, Neil – Thank you for putting up with me in 'book-writing mode' when my attention is too often diverted onto the job at hand; and for those times when you've helped me grapple with, and find my way through, the tricky bits! Thank you for picking up the extra chores when I was working long hours. Thank you for listening, for praying, for your unfailing support. Thank you for showing me God's love, patience and wisdom, time and time again.

And finally, thank You God, for that key moment when You whispered the name of Gideon into my heart, reassuring me that this book would happen if I depended on You implicitly for its completion. How true it is, that without You, I can do nothing (John 15:5).

Contents

Preface   8

Part One – A life out of balance
Recognising the imbalance   12
The Promised Land   20

Part Two – Restoring the inflow
Restoring the inflow – introducing the theme   28
Restoring the inflow – through God's Word   32
Restoring the inflow – through prayer   42
Restoring the inflow – of God's image   51
Restoring the inflow – through identity and worth   61
Restoring the inflow – through rest   71

Part Three – Restoring the outflow
Restoring the outflow – introducing the theme   82
Restoring the outflow – through *agape* love   88
Restoring the outflow – through witness   97
Restoring the outflow – through *charismata*   107
Restoring the outflow – through spiritual battle   115

Part Four – Restoring the balance beyond this book
To be a 'thin place'   126
Nurturing the 'thin place'   133
Taking possession of 'promised-land life'   142
Restoring the balance beyond this book   150

Endnotes   156

Preface

'The proof that we have the vision is that we are reaching out for more than we have grasped. It is a bad thing to be satisfied spiritually… Our reach must exceed our grasp… If we have only what we have experienced, we have nothing; if we have the inspiration of the vision of God, we have more than we can experience. Beware of the danger of relaxation spiritually.'
Oswald Chambers[1]

Your car has to have an annual MOT, your boiler needs to be serviced, you may even give your heart, eyes and teeth a regular check-up, but how is your walk with God? How would you describe the condition of your spiritual life? Is it vibrant, empowered and moving forward? Or is it sluggish, stagnant, disillusioned and buried beneath the busyness of life? Do you feel, for any reason, that you could use a spiritual health check?

Restoring the Balance is for women who feel that there is something lacking in their spiritual life, for women who long for a more meaningful connection with God every day, or for women who feel spiritually dry, who've plateaued in faith or hit a 'brick wall' and need help to move forward again.

It's for women who read about the Spirit-filled people of the Bible, and nurse a dream for the same degree of spiritual empowerment. But it's also for women struggling to keep afloat of frenetic schedules or stressful demands, whose engagement with God has been forced to sit on the side-lines. And it's for women disheartened by setbacks, discontent, confusion, disillusionment, mundane routines, pressing problems and pain; a season of life where heavenly realms and spiritual riches seem all too irrelevant to the reality of their today.

We may all be in different seasons of life, but many of us share the same problem. We know in our heads what we believe about God, but the life of His Spirit feels remote, detached or maybe even non-existent. Our Spirit-led lives are skewed out of balance by problems, discouragements, and demands that we sometimes face in life.

I first made a commitment to Jesus in my mid-teens, but my spiritual life was often out of balance with my life in the world whenever I neglected my devotion to God. I never lost my faith, but my belief wasn't born out in the way I was living: drinking, clubbing, inappropriate relationships and prioritising career goals above my relationship with God.

A few years later, I determined to get myself right with God even though I was settled in a long-term relationship with a man who did not share my faith. I recommitted my life, then prayed for the day when my man would love Jesus too. But as time passed and he remained unconvinced by the Christian faith, I sensed the Holy Spirit prompting me to break up the relationship in order to restore the fullness of living within His plan and purpose for my life. It was deeply painful for both of us. However, it was also a significant period of spiritual growth for me.

I was now a single woman with a heart and space to nurture quality times with God in prayer and His Word. But once again that harmony between the Holy Spirit and flesh skewed out of balance with my next season of life. I was invited to a charity fundraiser dinner by a man I vaguely knew from church and,

12 months to the day later, we married. It was a very exciting time and clearly God's will for me but when I became a wife and mother, I struggled to find time to maintain the balance of feeding my day-to-day life with spiritual input. And when my career became our sole source of income while my husband retrained for church ministry, pressure on time tipped that balance even more.

But it hasn't just been the demands of life that I've allowed to limit my experience of God in my everyday life; there have also been my fears and insecurities. I've said 'no' to God-given opportunities because I feared I just wasn't good enough, and I've held back from entering into full-time Christian ministry for fear that I wouldn't earn enough to pay into a government pension or cover future bills. This is just a snapshot of my life journey that birthed this book; a journey of learning how to restore the balance of the life of God's Spirit in me with my imperfect life in the world.

So, now I invite you to be honest about your own walk with God as I continue to share how I've grappled with faith in different seasons of my life. I will unpack helpful scriptures, offer practical guidelines, and give space for you to reflect and pray. I hope you will join me on my journey of growing dependence on Jesus, as we learn to apply our faith to whatever we face today, to our quest for meaning and purpose, or our longing to be further empowered and used for God's kingdom work.

Part One

A LIFE OUT
OF BALANCE

Recognising the imbalance

'I do believe; help me overcome my unbelief!'
(**Mark 9:24**)

It was Boxing Day, and I was walking the Welsh Clwydian hills, half-praying, half-mulling over my aspirations for the next 12 months: to pray more, to be a better friend, to finish my novel, to discipline those obstinate ungodly habits, to increase my giving of time, money and hospitality, to research an idea long brewing in my heart, to conquer that barren patch of the garden… They all sounded good in theory, but I knew from past experience that, once the holidays were packed away, reality would kick in and I would leap straight back into my usual routines. The inspiration and perspective of reflective time away would be quickly forgotten after a busy day trying to complete an endless list of 'to do's.

All these years later and I can still picture that muddy track, my family chattering in Christmas hats, and the skeletal beauty of winter trees scattered across the panoramic view as my thoughts were interrupted: 'Believe. Believe in me. Believe in my promises. Not just in your head but walking it out in *every* part of your life.'

My list of goals were all well and good, but God was prompting a new resolution: to engage with, depend on, respond to and so nurture the reality of my belief in Him at the core of my being. In other words, to live out what I said I believed wholeheartedly and to such an extent that, if God wasn't in controls, I could potentially end up falling flat on my face.

My attention was caught.

I paused to join my family sipping steaming mulled wine from flasks, while continuing to ponder on the nature of my belief. Yes, I'd had a genuine life-changing encounter with God in my early twenties, but in truth, I was still driven to some extent by fears and insecurities, by comfort and pleasure, by discouragement and doubt, by my own ambitions and cultural expectations. I believed everything I knew about God, but was not experiencing the fullness of His Spirit-life as Scripture suggested. And I wanted more. I longed to let God help me envisage life where I lived out my belief in full – engaging with God in every aspect of my day, and in every season of life.

The question still hanging over me while skidding down a slippery slope back to the car, was 'how?'

God never intended for belief to be limited to an intellectual knowing about, or talking about, Him. Christian belief needs to be lived out in practice. If our actions don't line up with our beliefs then our faith isn't as important, or life-forming, as we might like to think.

Belief in Jesus is our banner over life. It's the path we resolutely follow when others entice us to walk their way. It's our vision, our assurance, our goal and guidance for life. It is the presence of almighty God dwelling within us, shaping, resourcing and empowering – an awesome reality I refer to as 'Spirit-life' throughout this book.

True belief is therefore a living experience of God in our

day-to-day. It's not just knowing about spiritual blessings but encountering their impact and seeing them enrich our lives in the world. And Jesus modelled this perfectly, showing how the physical life can be in perfect harmony with the fullness of God's Spirit-life indwelling human flesh.

OK, so we're not Jesus, but we are united with Him; in fact we live *in* Him. I love how Paul never used the word 'Christian', but described believers as being 'in Christ', 'in the Lord', 'in God', 'in the heavenly realms'. In Christ we find every spiritual blessing made available to us, a continual flow of spiritual gifts that transcend but include the material.[2] We don't have to ask for them, we just need to appropriate them by faith; to turn our attention onto what is already ours, to enrich our lives in this world.

In John 10:10, Jesus promised life to the full. This wasn't a promise for endless problem-free happiness and prosperity, it was a promise of the fullness of God's Spirit-life impacting our life in the world. But life in this world can undermine our experience of that promise, which is why the story of Jesus healing a possessed boy in Mark 9:14–29 is intrinsic to restoring the balance of our belief. A father had asked the disciples to free his son of a destructive demon, but they had failed in their attempt. Disheartened by the experience, he approached Jesus, hoping, instead of confidently believing, in His ability to help. But Jesus worked with the man, transforming his head belief into an experience with the living God.

'I do believe; help me overcome my unbelief' (Mark 9:24) is a powerful prayer, and one we might all find helpful for different reasons. It's a prayer we're going to adapt and pray throughout this book, asking Jesus to help us turn from whatever distracts, discourages, or undermines us from believing in Him; whatever dilutes our experience of the fullness of God's Spirit-life imparting Himself in and through our physical life.

Jesus is heaven's presence to us right now, today. But sometimes we need to restore the balance of our openness to God, to 'become in daily experience what [we are] positionally in Christ.'[3] There may be times when we might find ourselves praying: 'Lord, I do believe my soul is alive in You, but heavenly realms and spiritual blessings sound all too surreal compared with meeting the mortgage repayments, coping with redundancy, caring for young ones, negative health test results, infertility issues, the unrelenting demands of my boss, suffering from a failed pension scheme, grieving a loved one, pain, distress and bewilderment… which are far more real to my daily tangible experience.'

So what do we mean by 'restoring the balance'?

'Balance' suggests a state of equilibrium or something that brings it about. It speaks of harmony in the parts of the whole. In our case, the balance we're aiming for is an equilibrium between the Spirit-life of God and the life we live in the world. It's learning how to engage with that 'something' – our divine inheritance – that will bring about harmony between Spirit and flesh. Restoring the balance will, therefore,

> 'the balance we're aiming for is an equilibrium between the Spirit-life of God and the life we live in the world.'

help us make Christ-empowered living in the world our daily experience, whatever our season or circumstances.

Some of us may need to restore the balance because we've grown disillusioned with faith by what we read in Scripture. We read that Jesus opened the mouth of a fish to find money to pay his taxes, and think, 'Yeah, great, but I have to work extra hours to pay my bills.' We read His command to go out into all the world, and think, 'Yeah, great, but I'm stuck indoors, isolated by physical limitations.' We read how Peter commanded the paralysed man to stand up and walk, and think, 'Yeah, great, but God doesn't manifest miracles in my life, church or community.' We read how Jesus got up early to pray or prayed right through the night, and think, 'Yeah, great, but my toddlers cling to my legs all day and refuse to stay in bed at night.' We read of promised peace and comfort and think, 'Yeah, great, but my troubles, fears and distress feel more real to me' or 'my distracting frenetic schedule leaves no time to engage with spirituality.' And we read of promised empowering and think, 'Yeah, great, but I feel so dry and God seems so aloof that spiritual riches sound more like a fairy-tale than the reality of my life of slog, and little if any "fruit" for God's kingdom.'

Some of us might need to restore the balance when we're being pulled in too many directions; when we've allowed personal interests and goals to overshadow our life in Christ. Some of us might need to restore the balance if we're feeling apathetic, sceptical even that spiritual matters have any real impact on life right now. Others of us may feel stuck in a rut; we long for a greater experience of a Christ-empowered life but it's just not happening. These are all valid reasons why our lives in this world may feel out of balance with God's Spirit-life in us. But we don't have to keep on living with that imbalance.

Life in Christ is lifted above the commonplace here and now, but is still very much a part of it. We have been set apart *from* this world for a holy purpose *in* this world. So, restoring the balance enables us to understand what's important in life; what to hold on to, and what we need to let go of – decluttering what might have become an overly busy schedule. It teaches us when to persevere for a season and when to say 'enough', when to keep depending on God's strength, and when to declare His authority over a situation. And it infuses our emotional wellbeing with a quiet but unshakeable confidence in who we are in God. Where once we might have struggled with body-image issues or lacked a sense of self-worth, restoring the fullness of God's Spirit-life instils a rooted security that we cannot source from anything or anyone else in this fallible, temporary world.

'We have been set apart *from* this world for a holy purpose *in* this world.'

Getting personal – making this real

'*We are not human beings having a spiritual experience; we are spiritual beings having a human experience*' J. John[4]

'The goal of engaging with spiritual blessings is not merely for our own wellbeing, though they do enrich life beyond measure! Our primary goal is that we may live 'to the praise of [God's] glory.' (**Eph. 1:14**)

— **Paul's longings and aspirations were born out of his life in Jesus rather than influenced by the world. What or who influences your aspirations for your life?**

'Praise be to the God and Father of our Lord Jesus Christ, who has blessed us in the heavenly realms with every spiritual blessing in Christ… I pray that the eyes of your heart may be enlightened in order that you may know the hope to which he has called you, the riches of his glorious inheritance in his holy people, and his incomparably great power for us who believe.' (**Eph. 1:3,18–19**)

— **What distracts you from the spiritual blessings that are available to enrich your life; for example, busyness, pleasures, pain, financial pressures, or apathy?**

'Since then, you have been raised with Christ, set your hearts on things above, where Christ is, seated at the right hand of God. Set your minds on things above, not on earthly things. For you died, and your life is now hidden with Christ in God.' (**Col. 3:1–3**)

— To aspire to 'things above' is to first meditate, dwell and intentionally engage with a Christlike life. How could you do that more?

— To 'set [our] hearts on' is to desire, look for, and seek to obtain. What is your heart set on?

— To 'set [our] minds on' is to think about, make it our attitude, and honour all that it stands for. What is your mind primarily occupied with? Would you like that to change?

Sometimes our life circumstances make it difficult for us to focus more on the kingdom of God, adopting its perspective and honouring all it implies, but let's be encouraged to preoccupy our hearts and minds on the life and purpose of Jesus.

Father God, I pray for a greater fullness of Your Spirit of wisdom and revelation, so that I may know You better. Lord, open the eyes of my heart that I may grasp the immense nature of my awesome spiritual inheritance in Jesus and the glorious empowering of Your Spirit-life, available to me, even while I continue to live in the world. Amen.

The Promised Land

'Now then, you and all these people, get ready to cross the River Jordan into the land I am about to give to them—to the Israelites. I will give you every place where you set your foot, as I promised Moses.' (**Josh. 1:2–3**)

Lord, I do believe in Your promise of 'life to the full' (John 10:10). I do believe in a harmony between Your Spirit-life and my natural life; Your abundant overflowing presence infusing, guiding and empowering me. But some of life's seasons make this harder to engage with than others, and, in the reality of life, I'm not sensing the fullness of my belief as promised. Lord, help me overcome this imbalance between what I know to be true in my head and what I'm experiencing in my 'today'. Amen.

A promised-land life for today

'The Promised Land' – what comes to mind when you hear that expression? Perhaps you're thinking about the land of Canaan, renamed Israel, described as 'flowing with milk and honey' (Exod. 3:8)? The land set apart for God's people where they could be at home with Him, and He with them. A place where they could become His blessing to all nations. Or perhaps you're thinking of the future; to our heavenly home

'a life on earth that is infused and empowered by God's Spirit.'

prepared for us to live with Jesus. But I'd like to suggest there can also be a 'promised land' for today: a life on earth that is infused and empowered by God's Spirit. And it's this pictorial metaphor we will keep in mind as we seek to restore that balance throughout this book.

God's promise of a land full of potential to sustain abundant life is on offer to each one of us, just as it was offered to Joshua and the 12 tribes. It is a promise of the fullness of God's Spirit-life infusing our physical life with 'milk, honey and abundant fruit' to nourish others as well as ourselves. But first we have to want it, choose it, and depend on God to help us take possession of it.

'Promised-land life' isn't free of problems, however. Just as the Israelites sweated and toiled to dig, plough and sow into the sun-baked soil, so work and life in this world can be tough. And just as they were harassed by pagan nations oppressing their borders, raiding their crops and, at times, domineering them, so we have a spiritual enemy who is always on the lookout to undermine our wellbeing, disrupt our work for the kingdom and exploit our weaknesses.

Neither is 'promised-land life' a place of self-effort and striving. It's a place of loving devotion: our soul's instinctive response on encountering Jesus. It's a place of being open and available to God; of surrender to the one who offers the only 'good thing' (Psa. 16:2) worth having: *His* love, *His* provision, *His* equipping, *His* honour, *His* character, *His* purposes and *His* influence. It's the place of God-given victory in Christ over our spiritual enemy. It's the place where we can impact the world in which we live through the power of our Father.

In short, 'promised-land life' is being at home with the Spirit-life of God, just as God wants to be at home in our lives in the

> '"promised-land life" is being at home with the Spirit-life of God'

world. So let's think about that for a moment as we picture the Promised Land of the Bible, and where we might now find ourselves on that metaphorical map.

Remaining on the east bank

Perhaps we're like the Gadites and Reubenites; two Israeli tribes who had as much right as the other ten tribes to God's inheritance on the west bank of the Jordan River, but on seeing that the lands on the east bank were adequate enough for their vast herds, they opted to stay put. They settled for second best, saying: 'let this land be given to your servants as our possession. Do not make us cross the Jordan' (Num. 32:5). God didn't condemn their choice, but in choosing to forego the fullness of the Promised Land and staying in a place that was merely sufficient, there were times when that second-best place made them more vulnerable to attack.

So what about us? Life in this world can be so attractive that we can become distracted by it, and so entrenched in busy schedules, personal goals and ambitions, relationships and treasured possessions, which we clutch so tightly that we never grasp a true love or 'first love' for God. It could be that we're just disinterested; life 'this side of the Jordan' is comfortable, happy, and provides all we think we want, so there is no perceived need for a greater fullness of God's Spirit-life on offer 'over the Jordan'.

Or maybe we're just too afraid to cross over: the waters are a raging flood, enemies roar on the opposite bank, and we don't know what the territory will be like on the other side. There are just too many unknowns in accepting more of the Spirit-life of God, too many insecurities – it is safer to stay where we are than to receive the fullness of our promised inheritance.

Living in Philistia

Perhaps we're like those who *have* crossed over but become so discouraged by problems that, like David when he ran away from Saul and took refuge in the land of the Philistines (1 Sam. 27), we've run away from trusting in God, compromised our devotion and entered into ungodly habits and relationships. Or perhaps we did cross over into the life we felt God calling us to, but the Spirit-filled harmony we once enjoyed has been undermined by the hard work required, lack of obvious fruit or frequent discouragements.

We're disheartened by other people's behaviour, like Moses was when the Israelite people made a golden calf. We have troubles so great that we're inclined to give up, like Elijah who was afraid and wanted God to take his life. Or like Jonah, we're so lacking in confidence that we're intentionally running in the opposite direction of God's leading; or we've let a negative attitude take root, holding us back from moving on with God. Sometimes our words, behaviour or priorities can, like Peter's, deny our professed belief, leaving us feeling guilty and isolated. Or else we're like Martha, struggling with such a hectic schedule that there's simply no time to just be with Jesus – to rest, listen, love, and be loved.

There are so many reasons why you may not be experiencing God's 'promised-land life' today. But my prayer for you is that as we continue to explore this theme your balance of life will be restored to the full.

Getting personal – making this real

'We are homesick for something that lies beyond the universe yet strangely affects our world. Our sense of regret points to a primordial homesickness – a sorrow that afflicts us precisely because we turn ourselves away from God who is the country we long for, the land of lost content… The saints have a raging sense of their need for God. He is the country of their soul, and tidings of that far country break in upon them. That is the meaning of Christ, who brought tidings, news of that country. He brought the very air of it into our land of exile.' Richard Holloway[5]

— **Picture how your life would look if it were filled with the fullness of God's Spirit-life equipping and empowering. How different does that appear to your life right now?**

— **Are you 'east of the Jordan'? What has dampened the passions of your heart for God, or lured you away from pursuing the best of your God-given potential?**

— **Are you 'in exile in Philistia'? Who, or what, disillusioned you in your journey of faith that you now find yourself in exile from the fullness of God's blessing?**

— **In what ways are you struggling in the 'Promised Land'?**

You may have faced fears that have chased you in the opposite direction to God's purpose for your life, or you might have known insecurities that have shackled you from pursuing the life God called you to. However, God's desire is for your natural life to dovetail with your spiritual life in Christ, and for you to come to a place 'flowing with milk and honey' so that you are enabled to bless others. I encourage you to place your fears and insecurities at His feet and let Him restore you.

> **Lord, I'd like to know more of this 'promised-land life' of abundant spiritual provision and influence. Help me hear You speak to my heart and situation, and learn how to restore the balance of Your glorious Spirit-life impacting my life in the world. Amen.**

Part Two

RESTORING THE INFLOW

Restoring the inflow —
introducing the theme

'the land you are crossing the Jordan to take possession of is a land of mountains and valleys that drinks rain from heaven. It is a land the LORD your God cares for; the eyes of the LORD your God are continually on it from the beginning of the year to its end.'
(**Deut. 11:11–12**)

The Promised Land of ample provision of milk, honey and fruit, of wholeness and wellbeing in God, and of being His blessing to others, was a land that endured a season of intensive dry heat. Long months of sunshine dried up seasonal 'wadis' or ravines that were only filled with water during the rainy season, and crops rooted in hard baked soil held out for God's blessing of life-giving rains, essential to harvests and herds. It was the rains that restored lush pastures from sun-burned wastelands, rejuvenated swathes of green alongside desiccated riverbeds, nourished wilting wheat and barley, surged down dusty gorges, replenished underground wells in the hills and refilled empty cisterns in the white limestone rock. And just as God's people relied on the blessing of rain to nourish and nurture their crops, we too rely on the outpouring of His Spirit to cultivate a 'promised-land life' in Him: the fullness of His Spirit-life flowing into our life in the world.

God's invitation to drink

As you survey your spiritual landscape, is it withered and parched? Are you thirsty for more of God's Spirit to rejuvenate your life? Jesus said, 'Let anyone who is thirsty come to me and drink. Whoever believes in me, as Scripture has said, rivers of living water will flow from within them' (John 7:37–38).

To drink of God's Spirit-life is to take it in; to assimilate 'the very life of God in Christ to the point where it becomes a part of [us].'[6] We can't earn God's favour and blessing, but there's a natural and supernatural principle at work – what we drink will give life to us. The question is: are we drinking deep of the life we have in Christ, or turning to polluted wells to satiate our thirst for love, guidance, significance or purpose? Jesus highlighted the futility of turning

'To drink of God's Spirit-life… will give life to us.'

to other wells to quench our thirst instead of drinking from His life-giving water. In John's Gospel, He stressed the importance of sticking close to Him. 'Remain in me, as I also remain in you. No branch can bear fruit by itself; it must remain in the vine. Neither can you bear fruit unless you remain in me. I am the vine; you are the branches. If you remain in me and I in you, you will bear much fruit; apart from me you can do nothing' (John 15:4–5).

It's this 'remaining' in Jesus that is the theme of Part Two; soaking up nourishment from His Word, drinking in His presence in prayer, maturing His life within us, establishing our worth in Him, and honouring His gift of life-giving rest are areas we will be exploring. As we remain in Jesus – immersing ourselves 'in Him' – God's Spirit impacts and transforms us, restores the balance of Spirit-life into our parched, pallid life in the world, enables us to experience Him in greater measure, and fulfils the awesome potential of bearing kingdom fruit.

Getting personal – making this real

> *'The true spiritual life is more than keeping away from bad habits and actions, or even doing good works… it means learning to abide in Christ. If we do not abide in Him then we will abide in something else.'* Selwyn Hughes[7]

— **What are you 'abiding' in? Where do your thoughts dwell?**
— **Where do your dreams find root and your soul search for life-giving water?**
— **How will you commit to focus your entire being on God's presence with you, His promises to you, and His longing to pour His Spirit into you?**

If you feel that you have not yet immersed yourself in God, and find yourself 'wishing' you had a deeper spiritual life, then remember that God never imposes Himself on you but if you come near to God, then He will come near to you. Christ's promise of life to the full is on offer for *you*. He is eager for you to accept it. James says: 'Say a quiet *yes* to God and he'll be there in no time. Quit dabbling in sin. Purify your inner life. Quit playing the field. Hit bottom, and cry your eyes out. The fun and games are over. Get serious, really serious. Get down on your knees before the Master; it's the only way you'll get on your feet.' (James 4:8–10, *The Message*).

Lord, I long to be saturated with Your life-essential water to renew, reshape and mature who I am, with an ever-increasing fullness of Your Spirit. Amen.

Restoring the inflow —
through God's Word

'In the beginning was the Word, and the
Word was with God, and the Word was God…
In him was life… The Word became flesh
and made his dwelling among us.' (**John 1:1,4,14**)

*Lord, I do believe Your Word is essential life-giving water, but I
don't have space to read it during my busy working week; parts of it
are confusing or boring. My children drain me of energy, so by the
time I flop into bed I'm far too tired to read. Help me to make time
with Your Word a reality in my day-to-day life. Amen.*

I don't know what inspired me to do it, whether it was my own
idea or the prompting of God's Spirit, but in my early twenties
while I was travelling the world for a year, including six months
with Youth With a Mission, I decided to only read my Bible during
that time away from home. And that's what I did. Aside from a
handful of obligatory course books, I read Scripture as I'd never
read it before. It rooted me in truth, equipped my mind, focused my
will, infused my soul, steadied unstable emotions, empowered my
spirit and captivated my heart. In short, I fell in love with it! That
was me in 'Mary mode' – sitting at Jesus' feet with time to listen
to Him. But since then, I've often found myself in 'Martha mode',
chasing my tail to fulfil my obligations with barely, if any, time to
be in God's Word.

So much more than words on a page

Scripture was never meant to stay on the page, or even just in our minds. It is living and active, God-breathed and useful, so that we may be thoroughly equipped. God's Word is a vital tool for teaching, correcting, resourcing and enabling us to know and serve our Father. It is a lamp and a light to guide and instruct, imparting wisdom and insight. It sees right through us, penetrating any outward façade or self-righteousness, to discipline and refine. The Bible sanctifies us, transforming our fallen nature increasingly into the image of the one who created us. It empowers us to resist and defeat spiritual powers; it revives and comforts; it is truth and a double-edged sword. In fact, references to the life-giving power of God's Word are just too many for this book!

So reading the Bible is not so much about the amount of time involved or the numbers of verses read, it's about being 'in Jesus' – who is the Word – and He in us. Being *in* the Word and letting the Word dwell *in* us helps us connect with God's presence as we still our thoughts and emotions in order to reflect and respond; letting the impact of God's message engulf our soul and infuse our physical being. It's that acute sense of God within the pages that changes Bible reading

'reading the Bible is… about being 'in Jesus' who is the Word and He in us.'

from being task-driven to relationship-driven. Rather than seeing it as something we *ought* to do, it becomes something we *long* to do. We become eager to experience its power to transform and equip us, infusing God's Spirit-life into the core of our being. But the extent to which we benefit from this empowering inflow is a choice we each have to make; one which may be affected by our current season of life.

Recognising the season

The writer of Ecclesiastes reminds us that there is 'a season for every activity under the heavens' (Eccl. 3:1) – even in 'promised-land life'.

As a new Spirit-filled Christian, I was excited at how the Bible, which I'd previously thought was dull and outdated, suddenly came to life. I was single with plenty of time to satisfy my hunger for more of God's Word. But that changed when a man started calling me 'wife', and a little girl 'mummy'; the quiet space I'd once enjoyed was rarely available. That season changed again when we moved to London in order for my husband to retrain and I became the family 'breadwinner', regularly working a 60-hour week in the city. I began to feel guilty about a perceived lack of commitment to reading my Bible, instead of accepting my changing circumstances and restoring the inflow of God's Spirit-life in ways that suited my new season of life.

From banker to pastor's wife, mummy to granny, fit and active to laid up sick, homemaker to administrator, writer to speaker, I've learned to ask that question: 'How can I maintain the balance of God's Spirit-life inflow in *this* season, without comparing myself to others in their own seasons of life, or feeling condemned when I can't sustain the pattern of reading I enjoyed in the past?'

There is a difference between reading for knowledge and reading for transformation. Both are good, but being able to read widely and for any length of time may not be possible in certain seasons of life. But mulling on, praying into, and proactively responding to a verse each week (or month) is possible in nigh on every season (except perhaps when health has so deteriorated that even that's not possible). Of course, only you will know if there are reasons that prevent you from giving quality time to your Bible, or if you're choosing to

'There is a difference between reading for knowledge and reading for transformation.'

fill available time with lesser priorities. But whatever your 'today' or season of life, I want to encourage you to let God's Spirit-life Word infuse your being in appropriate and realistic ways. In Colossians, Paul says, 'Let the message of Christ dwell among you richly' (Col. 3:16). The Amplified translation talks about the Word of Christ 'dwelling in your heart and mind—permeating every aspect of your being'.

'Dwell' means to live in, to remain as a permanent resident. It is God's desire to make His home in each of our lives, and as we make room for His Word, we welcome Him in as a permanent resident – to remain in and to permeate every part of us. He is with us, not just while we're reading the Bible but as we get on with our day.

'Richly' means in abundance, in an elaborate, plentiful way, fully, thoroughly and in full measure. To let the Word dwell richly on a daily basis suggests keeping a verse or passage in mind to guide, challenge, shape and inform our words, feelings, behaviour and priorities; letting God's living Word be formed in us, which, in turn, transforms our responses to people and situations in our everyday routine. And this can be life-changing in so many ways. It imparts God's peace, comfort, wisdom, guidance, confidence, discipline and hope – even in the darkest and most difficult of days. It roots the longings of our physical life in our Spirit-life; establishing us in the truth of God's love, character, purpose and power. You might be ready to agree with this idea in principle but wonder what it can look like in practice. Let me share with you a couple of my own experiences.

Worrying comes naturally to me, but it was during a period of particular stress that God instilled this Spirit-life Word to my anxious physical being: 'For the Spirit God gave us does not make us timid, but gives us power, love and self-discipline' (2 Tim. 1:7). I made it the background image on my laptop so that I couldn't help but be faced with the truth throughout my working day. The spirit of worry, fear and racing anxious thoughts is not from God, but comes from within ourselves and from the spiritual enemy. Longing to be freed from these ungodly anxieties, I chose to open my heart to this verse. By doing so, I was equipped and able to really appreciate His love for myself and others, and to receive a composed, ordered mind.

Often, when I'm disillusioned at how my expectations have not been met, or feel some kind of lack in my wellbeing, Psalm 16:2 shifts my perspective back onto the one and only truly good thing in my life: 'You are my Lord; apart from you I have no good thing'. This isn't just a memory verse that trips off my tongue, it is a truth that I was challenged to pray and reflect on for three weeks in May 1992; to engage and respond to its potential implications. And it's a truth I've repeatedly returned to ever since, to shift my perspective onto the one permanent, unchanging, infallible treasure in my life; the one who is so very much more than anyone or anything I know, love, pursue or possess. The one who *is* my life.

I once enjoyed a successful career in investment banking, but God has since led me through seasons of full-time motherhood, part-time administration work, and now, full-time freelancing as a writer and speaker. During these different periods of my life, using Psalm 90 as a basis of prayer has helped me to discern God's calling: 'Teach us to number our days, that we may gain a heart of wisdom… May the favour of the Lord our God rest on us; establish the work of our hands for us – yes, establish the work of our hands' (Psa. 90:12,17). This psalm is God's Spirit-life Word to me and builds my trust in His guidance and provision.

Whenever I feel the barb of a sniper's criticism, insult or sarcasm, or an attempt to manipulate and control, my natural reaction is to retaliate – and sadly, I often do. In such times, I recall these verses from Isaiah: 'In repentance and rest is your salvation, in quietness and trust is your strength… The fruit of that righteousness will be peace; its effect will be quietness and confidence forever' (Isa. 30:15; 32:17). These words help me to grow Christ's love for the sniper; to respond with His humility and temperance instead of arguing or answering back, while His assurance dispels any need to justify myself. God's Word is powerful in keeping my mind and heart right with Him, releasing me from my need to fight back, helping me to pray for the critic, and trust them into His care.

I hope these personal examples will give you a taste of

how engaging with God's Word can restore its life-giving properties into your daily experience, which might otherwise be overwhelmed by your life in the world. This isn't just a case of mind over matter. This is the Word being made flesh through God's Spirit-life empowering it into our lives. It is Jesus still living and working His life in and through us. 'Life to the full' may sound elusive when faced with the storms of the world, but as we choose to engage with God's life-giving Words, we can experience the abundance of spiritual life on offer in 'promised-land life'.

Conversely, to have little knowledge of the Bible can limit our perspective and response to the demands of life. We can become anxious or afraid when problems strike, discontent when disappointed, battered with doubt when our faith is mocked, fearful of rejection when we let God down, inadequate or useless when we look at others' success, bewildered when we need to make decisions, cowering or giving in to our battle with the enemy… and I could go on!

That is why the Bible is so much more than some comforting words on a page, a few favourite verses, or a strict list of dos and don'ts that we feel we can never live up to. It's why reading and responding to it need not be a chore or a guilt-induced 'should'. It is life-giving; transforming us increasingly into Christ's likeness, growing the mind of Christ in us, and equipping us for the life God intended.

Getting personal – making this real

> '*One of the ways we can nurture this knowing of God within ourselves is through the prayerful reading of, and meditation on, Scripture. God's presence breathes through the pages of the Bible in a way that makes it unlike any other text, and generations of readers down the ages have been astonished at its ability not only to speak of God but to somehow make God present in the reader's experience.*' Chris Webb[8]

It takes time to grow our reading muscles. Right now, we may only manage to concentrate for five minutes. Our schedules may need to be changed to provide more reading time, and it takes days, weeks, months then years to ingrain the Word ever deeper into our being. And some of us are simply not in a season of life that allows for extended reading. So here are some questions to reflect on and tips, which I hope will encourage, inspire or help you to restore the balance of God's Spirit-life through His Word.

— **'Do your best to present yourself to God as one approved, a worker who does not need to be ashamed and who correctly handles the word of truth' (2 Tim. 2:15). What would 'do your best' look like for you?**
— **What resources would help you to study the Bible: a more accessible translation; a study Bible; a Bible handbook or encyclopedia; commentaries as books or digital apps?**

> *'Keep this Book of the Law always on your lips; meditate on it day and night, so that you may be careful to do everything written in it. Then you will be prosperous and successful'* (**Josh. 1:8**).

— **How might meditation become a greater part of your understanding and response to restoring the inflow of God's Word into your life?**
— **What or who would suffer if you spent more time in God's Word?**
— **What or who would benefit if you spent more time in God's Word?**

We can't all give the same time or attention, or even intellectual understanding to the Bible. But we can all do what *we* can do, to grow deeper into its truths. It might not just be biblical resources you need, but the choice to make more time. Give thought to how you could realistically and practically do that. Five minutes of focused immersion in the Word is far better than 50 minutes of distracted skim reading. Just a verse a week to meditate on while you care for dependants or young children, struggle with your health, or are committed to a season of prolonged working hours, will impart God's Spirit-life to enrich, comfort, guide and support you. And above all, may you know how much God is longing to meet with you without any condemnation.

Jesus, Word of God, 'Open my eyes that I may see wonderful things in your law' (Psa. 119:18). Please increase the powerful presence of Your life in me. May what I read about You become real in my experience as Your Spirit-life increasingly fills me. Amen.

Restoring the inflow —
through prayer

'pray continually' (1 Thess. 5:17)

Lord, I do believe in the importance, intimacy and power of prayer but I'm struggling to make or find time. I feel disillusioned by past prayers that remain unanswered. I'm just too tired, upset, afraid, discouraged. Help me restore the inflow of Your Spirit-life through prayer as I learn to be present in Your presence; to give You my undivided attention, to still the rampaging thoughts and fears of my life in the world, and focus on being with You. Amen.

When I moved to London, I developed the habit of keeping a list of things I wanted to share or ask my mum about the next time we chatted on the phone. Mum also made a list, so we would take turns to ask questions or talk about something we'd done, but before we knew it, our time was up and goodbyes were said without really hearing what was on each other's heart. When she came to visit, however, we spent quality time over pots of tea, moving past the trappings of life to engage at a deeper level.

Pray continually? You must be joking!'

Prayer lists are a bit like that list I kept for Mum – a helpful prompt to inform our prayers and nudge a poor memory. So I'm certainly not against prayer lists, in fact I still use a few but no one can pray for everything. Feeling obliged, but unable, to pray for all the mountainous needs around us might leave us feeling inadequate or that we're not as spiritual as other Christians. And perhaps, more importantly, may distract us from the primary blessing of prayer, which is simply to engage with the presence of Jesus.

Paul teaches us to 'pray continually', one of the shortest verses with the biggest punch in the Bible, but perhaps also a teaching too easily misunderstood. The meaning of 'continually' here is not about mumbling prayers all day, but encouraging ongoing intimacy with God between set times of prayer; keeping the line of communication open to prompt further conversation.

Prayer is our Father's gift, enabling us to maintain the balance between our lives in Christ and our lives in the world. It can also be one of the things we most struggle to find time for, one way we become discouraged in our faith when prayers remain unanswered, or an area that might lead us to feel like we are second-rate Christians when we feel that we don't pray enough or with any obvious results.

So as we restore the balance of prayer in our lives, remember that it is first about relationship with God, about knowing Him and being known. Rather than being a task to be done, prayer helps us to focus on God's unseen presence, and trains our hearts and minds to be open to Him – whoever we are with and whatever we are doing. Restoring the balance of prayer isn't just about making time for a regular prayer slot, as that's not always possible for many women. First, it's about nurturing an awareness of God with us – and us with Him – throughout our day. Jesus remained attuned to His Father's presence whether He was alone up a mountain or being pressed to pass judgment on an adulterous woman; whether He was taking time out with His closest friends or crushed by frantic crowds eager for healing.

> 'prayer helps us to focus on God's unseen presence'

Yes, prayer happens alone at home, in church and mid-week meetings, but it's when we engage with mums at the school gate, with friends in the pub, or with colleagues at work that prayer becomes a constant drawing on the grace of God. It is our way of grappling with life with God, of living and engaging our physical life with His Spirit-life within. So let's aim to bring our whole lives into the orbit of prayer – the orbit of God with us, and in turn nurture our physical life with Spirit-filled prayer. Or as Philip Yancey suggests, to 'place ourselves in the stream of God's movement on earth'.[9]

Learning to be present with God

Some of us also might need to restore the balance of prayer in our private devotional space, be that as praise or proclamation, petition or spiritual battle, lament or intercession. A balance that can be skewed by the distractions and demands of life regardless of our current season. We can be in the same room as a person without talking to, listening to, or engaging with their heart. In fact, we can be in the same room but oblivious to their presence if we're so focused on something else.

Being present is so important – not least with and for Jesus, who is with us always. However, focused private prayer often feels impossible when we're bombarded and distracted with life, exhausted by schedules, or riddled with fear. But Jesus didn't just choose disciples to train them up for 'doing': first 'He appointed twelve that they might be with him' (Mark 3:14), so that they would have a 'continuous association and intimate fellowship with Jesus himself.'[10] Being with God is the essence of prayer that helps restore the balance of our spiritual and natural lives.

Focusing our heart, soul, spirit and mind in prayerful attention on Jesus, invites His Spirit to impart Himself into our inward being, which helps us to pick up the beat of God's heart. A heart that beats with love and longing to be known and loved in return. A heart that coveys wisdom and guidance to those who ask, and that longs to equip and empower us to continue His work in the world. A heart pouring out peace, comfort, guidance and courage into souls ready to receive. And it's this awareness of being with God that helps us catch the beat of His heart for ourselves as well as for others. David understood this when he prayed: 'One thing I ask from the LORD, this only do I seek: that I may dwell in the house of the LORD all the days of my life, to gaze on the beauty of the LORD and to seek him in his temple… My heart says of you, "Seek his face!"' Your face, LORD, I will seek' (Psa. 27:4,8).

'God's heart… that beats with love and longing to be known and loved in return.'

Do you suffer with a busy mind; distracting thoughts that infiltrate your quiet space with God? Try learning to discern the important from the barrage of unnecessary busy-busy thoughts, and keep a notepad to jot down those things you don't want to forget. As for those unimportant thoughts, do what Jesus did with the storm and command them to be 'Quiet! Be still!' (Mark 4:39). Don't just say it in words, but turn your focus away from those thoughts to gaze on Jesus. You might even find it helpful to whisper His name, reminding yourself that He's with you. Above all, ask God to focus your mind and heart, to quiet your emotions and spirit, and to dismiss any distractions. He wants to hear from you no matter what you are feeling or what it is about.

In Ephesians, we read, 'pray in the Spirit on all occasions with all kinds of prayers and requests' (Eph. 6:18). There is no point feeling guilty for not praying about *abc* when God has burdened and impassioned your heart to pray for *xyz*. We are clearly instructed in Scripture to pray about certain areas: for those in authority, for willing hearts to share the gospel, for people in trouble, for those who need healing, and for persecutors of the faith. But there will also be things God burdens *your* heart to be praying for, which are different to those He has entrusted to others. So, if you're feeling dragged down by the impossibility of having too much to pray for, ask God to show you how He has called *you* to pray, then let go of the prayer burden He has given to others. When someone asks you to pray for them, a good idea is to offer to pray in the moment, or, if inappropriate, as soon as possible afterward. The same goes for prayer requests you might receive by text or email. God will guide you as to whether or not to keep praying for them. You might also feel that they might benefit from sharing with another person who has been in a similar situation, in which case suggest that to them.

Then begin your prayers with thanks and worship. Pausing in a busy world and work-centred life to focus on your life in Christ helps to magnify God's thoughts and ways above your own, which in turn puts the world and its problems back into perspective, helping you discern God's love, faithfulness, justice and Word for you. It stills the temptation to dictate to God what you think He should do, and listen to how He wants you to pray in line with His love and purpose.

'listen to how He wants you to pray in line with His love and purpose.'

You might also find it helpful to picture being yoked with Jesus – a wooden crosspiece fastened to both of your shoulders and attached to a plough. This helps you remember that you are not praying alone. It isn't a one-sided conversation; you pray in partnership with Jesus, asking His Spirit to guide your thoughts in how to plough prayers for God's Spirit to move in this world.

Of course, you can still be honest with God and share your own longings and feelings, and there will most certainly be times when you'll be praying without discerning His clear direction, but God doesn't want you to pray 'blind' – He wants you to pray 'in' the Spirit and to open the spiritual eyes of your heart to see life from His perspective.

And finally, an often-quoted verse from Mark's Gospel about prayer is: 'Whatever you ask for in prayer, believe that you have received it, and it will be yours' (Mark 11:24). There are many awesome promises about prayer, but their fulfilment isn't always the reality of our experience. We might say: 'I've asked, I've believed, but I *haven't* received,' and we grow discouraged in prayer. It's helpful to read biblical promises in context and not just as snippets; to see how they fit in the context of the passage and, indeed, the broader message of the Bible. Furthermore, be open to any need to confess and get yourself right with God, then consider whether the prayer request fits with Christ's love, character and purpose.

There are many other reasons why your prayers may not be answered as you'd hoped; for example, God's timing, spiritual warfare, freedom of choice, not being in the centre of God's will, or having to learn to depend on Him more despite an ongoing problem. But if you are feeling disheartened, then please don't forget that God cares for you. His apparent silence doesn't mean He doesn't care about how you feel. We pray to an all-knowing, all-loving compassionate Father, who longs to comfort and strengthen you.

Getting personal – making this real

'*How can there be intimacy with one who is waiting for us to fulfill a quota of prayer-work?... What if God does not demand prayer as much as gives prayer? What if God wants prayer in order to satisfy us? What if prayer is a means of God nourishing, restoring, healing, converting us? Suppose prayer is primarily allowing ourselves to be loved, addressed and claimed by God? What if praying means opening ourselves to the gift of God's own self and presence? What if our part in prayer is primarily letting God be giver? Suppose prayer is not a duty but the opportunity to experience healing and transforming love?*' Martin L. Smith[11]

— **How are you encouraged to 'pray continually'?**

We have no better teacher on prayer than Jesus. Pray the Lord's Prayer below slowly, line by line, considering the implication of each significant word or phrase, and responding to God as you feel led (see Matt. 6:9–13).

'Our Father in heaven,'
— **Reflect and respond to God as Father – a perfect heavenly Father.**

'hallowed be your name,'
— **How do you feel prompted to revere and respect Him in prayer?**

'your kingdom come, your will be done, on earth as it is in heaven.'
— **How can you pray that your life in this world would increasingly align with God's kingdom purposes?**

'Give us today our daily bread.'
— **What are your needs as opposed to your 'wants'? Material? Spiritual? Emotional?**

'And forgive us our debts'
— **Allow time for the Holy Spirit to convict you of wilful or unintentional words, actions or habits that grieve Him.**

'as we also have forgiven our debtors.'

— **Forgive others by name; asking God's Spirit-life to fill you with His love and grace toward them.**

'And lead us not into temptation,'

— **What are your weaker, vulnerable areas? Ask God's help to inspire you to stand firm against their enticement.**

'but deliver us from the evil one.'

— **A powerful prayer in the name of Jesus, when you sense the oppression of the enemy over your life or a situation.**

Lord, I want to connect with You. I've got so much I need or want to pray about, but right at this moment my mind is so achingly full and busy that I'll just name those thoughts then leave them with You, so that I can be still and know You with me. [Name them now, then be still…]

Restoring the inflow — *of God's image*

'"Let us make mankind in our image, in our likeness"… So God created mankind in his own image, in the image of God he created them; male and female he created them.'
(**Gen. 1:26–27**)

Lord, I believe You long to restore Your divine image which has been marred and undermined by my imperfect self. Help me overcome the selfish traits that fester and fight back in my natural responses, masking and impairing Your Spirit-life in me. Amen.

I am fortunate to have known, or known about, my parents and grandparents. I've inherited my dad's large brow and teeth, my mum's quick-to-suntan skin and arthritic big toes, my maternal granny's love of gardening and my paternal grandpa's musical gifts. Paternal granny shaped my slim neck and shoulders, but I'm rather relieved I didn't inherit maternal grandpa's ears! I could go on, looking for signs of that family image sculpted by the millions of genes that shaped my physical life, but in one respect I was created like everyone else, including you: created in the image of God – not in form or features of course, but in sharing God's nature and character.

God's moral disposition, His righteousness and holiness, love and justice, truth and wisdom were implanted into our created

> 'God longs to restore us into His likeness, into His perfect image made visible in Jesus.'

being. Sadly, His awesome image in us has been scarred and disfigured by sin. Niggly habits and attitudes grow and domineer such as critical opinions, swollen egos, greed, gossip, anger or impatience, which skew the balance of God's image in the life we live in the world. But God longs to restore us into His likeness, into His perfect image made visible in Jesus. As we open ourselves to the inflow of His Spirit-life, our values, attitudes and behaviour are increasingly transformed as the fullness of His character develops in our lives. This is the maturing of what Paul calls 'the fruit of the Spirit' – God's 'love, joy, peace, forbearance, kindness, goodness, faithfulness, gentleness and self-control' (Gal. 5:22–23).

Sometimes we can misunderstand the nature of spiritual fruit, trying but failing through self-effort to nurture it. For years I strived to be more Christlike; to 'grow' His character in my own strength; to ripen the innate imprint of my creator's image. But fruit, natural or spiritual, cannot swell or ripen without the right environment. I couldn't do it alone; my need to depend on God's Spirit-life was vital. Although most people show glimpses of God's image by being patient, kind or good, we cannot restore God's image in us without the one who first breathes Spirit-life into our soul. As it says in John: 'Flesh gives birth to flesh, but the Spirit gives birth to spirit' (John 3:6).

Yielding to the inflow

Jesus said, 'The kingdom of God has come near. Repent and believe the good news!' (Mark 1:15). 'Repent' implies a complete change of mind and heart as we turn away from one thing, and onto something else; as we turn our focus, thoughts, affections, priorities and responses onto Jesus. Repentance is a profound reorientation of our perspective from one that is immersed in the cold shadows of self, to one that basks in the light and warmth of our life in Christ. And it's that turning our attention on Jesus that changes our outlook on life because we start seeing it from God's higher perspective. We now look at life through a spiritual lens, which in turn inspires holy responses and actions.

> 'turning our attention on Jesus… changes our outlook on life'

I'm not perfect, nor ever will be this side of heaven, but here are a few examples of how turning towards Jesus, and nurturing the fruit of the Spirit, has helped me.

The fruit of the Spirit is:

Love

When I feel smug or sense my hackles rise as my heart turns cold towards a person, I urge myself to turn away from these feelings and see the individual from God's perspective, to discern His heartbeat for them and respond accordingly.

We will look at this in more detail in Part Three, but turning our thoughts to how God has loved us, helps us in turn to love others.

Joy

When I'm upset or grieving due to a broken dream, a lost identity, the company of a loved one, I choose to turn my heart to Jesus and the stillness of His powerful presence in and around me embracing me as I weep, comforting me deep in my inner core where the comforts of this world cannot reach.

It's as we let go of our treasures in the world that our soul can hold fast to God, and be filled with Spirit-life joy.

Peace

When I feel anxious about health, finances, work deadlines, problems in my family or church, it is the turning of my mind to God's promises in His Word that impart His peace to my soul.

God's Spirit-life peace isn't found in the things of the world, it transcends the natural and our understanding. True peace is only found in God.

Forbearance

When another driver cuts me up on the road, I turn my attention away from my irritation and onto God's love for that person. I pray for their safety and that of other drivers, that they will be prompted to take more care, or that God will be with them if they're struggling with a difficult day.

Rubbing shoulders with other imperfect people is bound to spark indignation, frustration or reactionary anger, but as God continues to extend His grace toward us, so we can allow His Spirit-life in us to mirror His grace to the world.

Kindness

When I'm frustrated or agitated by someone's behaviour, I count to ten as I turn my soul away from a potential hostile reaction, and onto God's benevolence for me and His world. God is sovereign with the right to act or judge, based on His higher ways and thoughts; a truth that reconnects my heart on His kingdom values.

As we refuse to pass judgment but turn our attention onto the needs and struggles of others, apparent or disguised, our life in Christ can't help but respond in some way that might lift their load.

Goodness

Even when it's easy to ignore or pass by a needy situation, I challenge myself to turn my heart, time and will to God, and discern how I can put His love into action.

We are called to perform good deeds, sometimes when it's inconvenient to us, or in ways that others might think are futile. But we do so not to earn God's favour or the admiration of others, but to emulate our Father who is intrinsically good.

Faithfulness

When I feel like cutting corners, shirking a task or giving up on God's purposes, I turn my thoughts to Christ's faithfulness to me; a powerful motivation to be steadfast and dependable like Him.

Faith is a belief to be worked out in practice; living lives of integrity, authenticity, commitment, dependence and response to the one in who we have put our faith.

Gentleness

When a storm of emotion or reactionary response threatens to engulf me, turning my thoughts to the behaviour of Jesus in the Gospels prompts me to choose to act with care and consideration for all people, at all times and in all circumstances.

We have no one to impress but our Father; we have no need to assert ourselves. Knowing that God is in control of our lives nurtures contentment, which is the ideal environment for His Spirit to grow His gentle character in us.

Self-control

When we feel the urge to behave in ways that oppose the Spirit-life of God, let's turn *away from rash actions, remind ourselves that our 'bodies are temples of the Holy Spirit' (1 Cor. 6:19), and act accordingly. We can honour God by not submitting to unhelpful cravings; engaging with His indwelling Spirit will help us to overcome.*

'let's say "yes" to a greater fullness of God's Spirit.'

Self-control means saying 'no' to immediately gratifying our selfish appetites. Instead, let's say 'yes' to a greater fullness of God's Spirit.

To restore the inflow of God's image is to turn away from self-pity, and towards His love when we feel needy of attention. It's to turn away from lack of concern, and towards God's heart for the poor, oppressed, prisoner and refugee. It's to turn our focus away from our debilitating confusion, and make a conscious effort to turn it towards the guiding truth and wisdom in God's Word – even if this takes time. It's to turn our attention away from self-motivated striving for success, popularity, position or power, and towards God's kingdom priorities.

Growing spiritual fruit is a whole deal more than a mere attempt at being nicer Christians. Restoring the inflow of God's image imparts to our physical lives the richness of God's love, joy and peace, an inward assurance and poise whatever we face in life, as well as wisdom to guide.

We are in Christ and Christ is in us: that is the balanced life of flesh and Spirit, which God invites us to nurture. The inflow of God's Spirit-life can help us answer questions such as:

- Can I or can't I do this and still glorify God?
- Should I or shouldn't I do that if I want to honour my Lord?
- As Christ's representative on earth, how should I speak to this person?
- How can I authentically represent my life in Christ in this relationship and situation, in this goal I am pursing or in my response to this person?

There might be many more questions we are faced with regarding how to live out our faith, but through the transforming power of the inflow of His Spirit-life, the image of God is reshaped in our lives and we are able to reflect who He is to the world.

Getting personal – making this real

'To give God the service of the body and not of the soul, is hypocrisy; to give God the service of the soul and not of the body, is sacrilege; to give him neither, atheism. But to give God both, is worship.' Based on the works of Stephen Charnock[12]

— **In what, if any, ways might you have allowed ungodly characteristics, habits, priorities, attitudes, values or behaviour to maintain a foothold on your life in Christ?**

Although it is not easy, Paul encourages us to turn away from old habits. 'You were taught, with regard to your former way of life, to put off your old self, which is being corrupted by its deceitful desires; to be made new in the attitude of your minds; and to put on the new self, created to be like God in true righteousness and holiness' (Eph. 4:22–24).

The cross says we are loved just as we are, not as we should be. Our salvation was sealed by God's Spirit the moment we said 'yes' to Jesus. To feel condemned is not of God's Spirit. God convicts and disciplines us for our good that we may share in His holiness. So stand against any feelings of shame, blame or disapproval; instead open your heart to His gentle but precise discomforting of your conscience, and ask Him to show you what needs to be put right.

'For God did not call us to be impure, but to live a holy life' (1 Thess. 4:7). Though God calls us individually to different tasks and relationships, we are all called to be holy – to live lives distinguishable from the world by our priorities and behaviour.

— **How does it make you feel knowing that you are holy because the Spirit of God lives in you? What changes might that suggest to the way you live?**

All the fruit of the Spirit are made one in love, for love is intrinsic to God's character. Below is the familiar passage from 1 Corinthians, which is often read at weddings. I have inserted 'Jesus' and 'He' where it reads 'love' and 'it':

> '*[Jesus] is patient, [Jesus] is kind. [He] does not envy, [He] does not boast, [He] is not proud. [He] does not dishonour others, [He] is not self-seeking, [He] is not easily angered, [He] keeps no record of wrongs. [Jesus] does not delight in evil but rejoices with the truth. [He] always protects, always trusts, always hopes, always perseveres. [Jesus] never fails*' **(1 Cor. 13:4–8)**.

— **What does this say to you about Jesus' love for you?**
— **Now insert your name in the passage above. How does that inspire your expression of Jesus' love to others? How does that challenge you?**

Reflect on the other fruit of the Spirit: joy, peace, forbearance, kindness, goodness, faithfulness, gentleness, self-control.

— **How have you been encouraged, comforted and supported when these characteristics have been shown to you by God, or by someone else?**

Prayerfully consider how God may want to encourage, comfort and support others through His fruit in your life. Perhaps certain names or faces come to mind as you pause to consider the nature of these godly characteristics. Be encouraged that you bring the awesome presence of Jesus to those you meet in your day; a presence to honour, but also a presence to enrich your life, and to be enjoyed by those you meet.

> **Jesus, I long to experience greater fullness of Your Spirit in my life, not only for my own comfort but to represent You better in my relationships and day-to-day activities. Search me and show me how I may work with You to grow Your image in me that I might fulfil my role as Your ambassador. Amen.**

Restoring the inflow — *through identity and worth*

'For in him we live and move and have our being.' (**Acts 17:28**)

Lord, I do believe that You love, value and accept me, that You desire and delight to work through me as Your Spirit equips and anoints. But my insecurities, sense of inability, and perceived lack of significance withhold me from being the person You created me to be and from fulfilling my potential. Help me clear the clutter so that You can fill me with Your truth. Amen.

Life bombards us with messages informing us of someone else's opinion about who we are; judgments on our capability, achievements, appearance or significance. But when we let such messages define our identity and inform our sense of self-worth, it skews the balance of our true identity and worth in Christ.

In my youth I struggled with a lack of self-worth. Being ridiculed for my newfound Christian faith; failing exams in subjects I only chose to please significant others; the devaluing, upsetting and traumatic repercussions of repeated unfaithfulness from one boyfriend and the mental, emotional and physical abuse from another, were all experiences that undermined my sense of worth to such an extent that I developed anorexia. For many years, I lived with the labels 'inadequate' and 'imposter'.

As an adult, I let my banking career define who I was. So when I resigned to be at home to bring up my daughter, I lost my sense of identity overnight. But instead of re-establishing it in God, I subconsciously re-rooted it in being her primary carer and confidante. Then later, when she got married and left home, I once again lost a chunk of my perceived significance and purpose in life.

Low self-esteem can often be linked to beliefs that we are incompetent, incapable, worthless, unworthy, unimportant, a failure, unlovable or unlikeable. These beliefs may result in us being gripped by guilt, fear, shame or even self-hatred, lacking in confidence or driven by perfectionism.

But God loves us as a doting parent loves their baby, before they've ever said or done anything to earn that love, because there's a part of Him within us. Unlike flowers, food, animals or birds, we were created in His image. No matter what we have done or how we feel, God loves us. It is very easy to believe the messages that we'll be liked, loved, popular or regarded acceptable provided we look, behave or achieve in a prescribed way. However, we risk projecting that subtle but powerful belief onto our understanding of our relationship with God. How He must weep when we let a world-view definition of love and acceptance overrule His truth.

> 'How He must weep when we let a world-view definition of love and acceptance overrule His truth.'

I am loved

We can try and *be* a 'somebody' – someone with a certain amount of significance, value and popularity – by aiming to have the 'right' body shape, wearing the 'right' fashion, achieving certain benchmarks of success, earning a certain wage. When these things elude us, however, then we fail to *feel* like a 'somebody'. Alternatively, as we accept that God's love is not just something to believe in, but releases us to be all we are in Him, we can *know* we are a 'somebody' to the one whose opinion is most important of all – our heavenly Father.

Personal identity is based on who a person is, and in God's view, all people are loved. However, accepting the implications that we are loved by God needs to be believed and adopted. Furthermore, personal identity seeks to answer the big questions, such as 'Who am I?' The Bible answers that question by saying that we are loved, valued, significant and created with purpose.

If we feed our identity by comparing our abilities to those of our friends and peers (how well we parent our children, our job success, attractiveness and popularity, or from one of the many cultural expectations of life in this world) then the source of our identity will ebb and flow with time, circumstances, imperfections, fallibility, ageing or when someone significant to us has died. This possibly affects our sense of worth too, as we learn that we can never quite be 'good enough', at least not on a permanent basis. Rooting ourselves in God's love and living out of it, however, nurtures contentment, peace, calmness of mind and confidence to be who He made us to be. Where once we might have craved to look like someone else and achieve what they have achieved, now we are inspired to be the person God created us to be. And where once we might have let fear, shame or a sense of inadequacy hold us back from fulfilling our God-given potential, now we are assured and emboldened to obey and pursue His calling.

Contentment in God's love refocuses our attention on letting Him grow His image in us and empower us for His purpose. It imbues wisdom, dignity and grace when confronted with challenging individuals or circumstances. It encourages us to step out and co-operate with His design for our lives so that God can work through us. We enjoy and are energised by His presence in all that He calls us to be and do.

Re-rooting yourself in who you are in God

'My people have committed two sins: They have forsaken me, the spring of living water, and have dug their own cisterns, broken cisterns that cannot hold water.' (**Jer. 2:13**)

Israel's hills are littered with water storage cisterns, either naturally occurring or dug out of limestone and plastered, without which in Bible times, the inhabitants would have struggled during the long summer months of dry heat.

Our spiritual lives need water as much as our physical lives, but I wonder if we're tempted to search for a life-source outside of God's love; to dig our own 'cisterns' – leaky fallible ones. Some of us look to the 'cistern' of praise and affirmation for a task well done, of being needed by others, or of being admired for our appearance. But if no one acknowledges us after we've hit that deadline at work, provided hospitality, or adopted a new hairstyle, we can feel overlooked and unimportant. Similarly, if children leave home and we are not needed so much as a parent, it can undermine our identity and sense of significance in God's kingdom work.

Our belief in our worth can plummet, and often our openness to God's Spirit-life too, so let's remember what Jesus said: 'Let anyone who is thirsty come to me and drink' (John 7:37), and drink deeply from Him instead of looking to our own potentially polluted 'cisterns' to meet our need for love, affirmation and purpose. Then hear again God's invitation to our soul: 'Come, all you who are thirsty, come to the waters… that your soul may live' (Isa. 55:1–3).

Not only do we need to drink from the right 'cistern', but we also need to accept who God made us to be. In Psalm 139 we read, 'For you created my inmost being; you knit me together in my mother's womb' (Psa. 139:13). God created us in the womb with natural attributes, with a gene pool, upbringing and God-created physical traits and qualities to serve His purpose. God created us with *today* in mind, to fulfil His purpose in *this* generation of which we are a part. 'For we are God's handiwork, created in Christ Jesus to do good works, which God prepared in advance for us to do' (Eph. 2:10).

Sometimes we might wish we were someone else or hanker for different gifts and abilities, but to do so is to be unfaithful to who God made us to be. Paul reminds us that God distributes spiritual gifts such as wisdom, prophecy and interpretation of tongues 'just as he determines' (1 Cor. 12:11). So instead of envying the gifts of others or trying to be their clone, let's be inspired by them, be true to who we are and the best version of who God made us to be.

Finally, let's choose to compare ourselves only with Jesus. He is our benchmark for character and purpose. Hebrews encourages us to fix 'our eyes on Jesus, the pioneer and perfecter of faith' (Heb. 12:2). Jesus is our true role model, and the one whom we should look to imitate. As God's children, we are encouraged to adopt His godly values, attitudes and behaviour, but often we are tempted to compare ourselves with others, something Paul clearly teaches is 'not wise' (2 Cor. 10:12). If we compare and consequently feel superior to someone else, we can feel proud, self-righteous, and potentially develop a brash, unattractive ego. Alternatively, as a result of comparing, we might feel inferior to someone else's attractiveness or ability and our self-worth is undermined.

> 'Jesus is our benchmark for character and purpose.'

So let's decide right now to put a stop to comparing, because we are made in God's image. This is the only family image to nurture and aspire to, which is revealed through Jesus perfectly in the Gospels. Of course, our character or image will never be perfect until we are fully transformed in eternity, but being 'transformed into his image with ever-increasing glory' (2 Cor. 3:18) is a God-given benchmark to aspire to.

Furthermore, when we believe 'I'm not…', God's name is 'I am!' When we think we're not good enough, God says, 'I am enough.' When we don't feel able, God says, 'I am able.' When we don't feel loved, God says, 'I am love.'

Let's stop comparing God's calling on others, and compare where we are with His calling on us – His purpose, enabling and provision. As Paul says, 'Make a careful exploration of who you are and the work you have been given, and then sink yourself into that. Don't be impressed with yourself. Don't compare yourself with others. Each of you must take responsibility for doing the creative best you can with your own life' (Gal. 6:4–5, *The Message*).

Getting personal – making this real

> '*Love is not dependent on our actions but is a condition of being.*
> *We learn to reside habitually in the Kingdom of God's love.*
> *And in that sphere of existence we feel God's smile and hear*
> *God singing over us, and our hearts are "strangely warmed."*
> *We no longer need the world's approval to feel valid.*'
> James Bryan Smith[13]

In the Song of Songs, the beloved describes herself as 'Dark am I, yet lovely' (Songs 1:5). Unlike other royal ladies, she did not have fair skin, which was an esteemed mark of beauty in the ancient world. However, her lover didn't care that she didn't meet the cultural standards of her day because he loved her. 'You are altogether beautiful, my darling; there is no flaw in you' (Songs 4:7).

— Imagine those words from Songs 4:7 being spoken to you by God, who loves you and created you. How does that make you feel?
— Are you comfortable or uncomfortable with your appearance? What perceived flaws stop you believing, accepting and receiving God's passionate love for you?

Be encouraged to receive God's love as genuine, and let that awesome truth inspire your thanks and praise.

— **In Isaiah we read, 'Yet you, LORD, are our Father. We are the clay, you are the potter; we are all the work of your hand' (Isa. 64:8). Picture yourself as the clay and the Lord as your potter shaping you for His intended purpose. How does that make you feel?**

As I wrote in my book, *The Mirror That Speaks Back*, 'The intimacy between potter and clay already exists, even in its state of formation. He will always love that jar, even with its potential weaknesses. No matter if sickness and ageing mar its form when it enters the heat of the kiln, its intrinsic value and purpose will never be changed.'[14]

— **What names have you given yourself, or allowed others to give you, that contradict with what God says, and feels, about you?**
— **Is God's love for you at the root and heart of your identity? Or do you look to someone or something else?**

Maybe you need to receive and accept the truth of how much God delights in you. For example, if you feel your name is Unworthy, God says you are worth even the life of His Son; if you feel your name is Inadequate, God says you are capable for all that He wants to work through your life; if you feel your name is Failure, God says you can do everything He has called you to in

His strength and love; and if you feel your name is Unattractive, God says you are His beautiful creation.

— **Read the following names that you have in Jesus. Which resonate most with you as a truth you need to claim?**
  I am *precious*
  I am *loved*
  I am *valued*
  I am *free*
  I am a *friend* of Jesus
  I am a *child* of God
  I am *accepted*
  I am a *temple* of the Holy Spirit
  I am a *new* creation
  I am an *heir* of God
  I am *chosen* by God
  I am God's *handiwork*
  I am a *citizen* of heaven
  I am *redeemed*
  I am *forgiven*

As we root our perception of ourselves in God's love, and nurture our responses out of His love, we will experience the wonderful truth that God is *always* for us. Let's open our hearts fully to His healing, transforming love, and so restore complete wholeness to our being.

Lord, I want to root and establish my whole sense of being in You. To let Your love, truth and purpose flow in and out through me; to hear clearly Your heart's desire both for my life and the lives of others. Amen.

Restoring the inflow —
through rest

'Remember the Sabbath day by keeping it holy. Six days you shall labour and do all your work, but the seventh day is a sabbath to the LORD your God. On it you shall not do any work' (**Exod. 20:8–10**)

Lord, I do believe in Your gift of rest; help me make that happen despite the pressure to keep going to fulfil all my duties, and the burdens of my soul that distract, drain and undermine with their niggling unease. Amen.

I'm tired. Right now, right in this moment as I begin writing this chapter, I'm tired. I'm not just talking tiredness from late or sleepless nights – though both have certainly played their part in recent weeks. I'm not just talking physical tiredness from running a marathon – I haven't, but that's how my body feels right now. And I'm not just talking tiredness from working excessively long days – though I've certainly had far too many of those in recent months.

Neither am I just talking tiredness from the burdens of my soul: of how to be present for my husband's needs during this busy phase; of living too far away from my daughter to be able to help with my grandsons as much as I'd like; of the care for ageing parents; of the persistent battle against a sense of shame and inadequacy; of church leadership responsibilities; and of a home and garden crying out for attention.

I'm talking about an exhaustion born from all of these factors and more. My body, mind, emotions and soul are spent. But I'm not trying to have a pity-party. I'm sharing with you the irony of dragging bushed-out-me to my desk to write a chapter on rest! Many of you reading this will be familiar with this kind of tiredness. Bless you, sister – I feel your fatigue but there is hope.

The fourth commandment is an encouragement to keep the Sabbath holy. God wants to lead us to places of rest that refresh our souls. Jesus called the weary and burdened to come to Him for rest, and He made space for His disciples to get rest. We also know that God created our body and soul with a need to rest in order to function at our best, but it's not always so easy to put these beliefs into practice.

Number one on the to-do list

God created everything we know, enjoy and pursue, but instituted a rhythm of work and rest, which He Himself modelled from the beginning of time; a rhythm we inherited when He made us in His image. Too much work and not enough rest can raise blood pressure, disrupt the digestive system, weaken immunity, trigger headaches, lead to muscular pain, or damage our wellbeing through stress, anxiety, depression or a sense of being overwhelmed. However, when we rest in line with how God designed our bodies, we return to work restored to peak efficiency.

Rest helps us to be present for people, spend time with them, and reach out to them with love; building relationship instead of tearing it down with tired irritability or distracted busy minds. Rest allows our body to stretch limbs out of office chairs, relieve eye strain from computer screens, revive muscles from hard labour and brains from mental fatigue. Rest also helps us take a step back to get a broader perspective when we've become so absorbed in our schedules that we've lost sight of where we are going and why.

There's a key difference between taking a day off from the perspective of our physical life and taking a sabbath rest for our spiritual life. The first is all about 'me': catching up with laundry, shopping and housework, or chilling out with TV. But sabbath rest is all about God's Spirit-life living in harmony with our physical life in the world; about honouring and depending on God, acknowledging how He made us, and cherishing time to simply enjoy His presence.

To keep one day as holy is to distinguish it from what we do the other six days of the week; from the interference that deafens us to God's whispers; from the busy routines that intrude on our enjoyment of Him; from the demands and expectations that are essential to working 'promised-land life' but which drain our mental, physical, spiritual and emotional resources; and also from the blaming, shaming and failing, which undermines the truth of who we are in Christ. Sabbath is not just permission to rest work-weary bodies, it is a gift: a God-given opportunity to make space to turn our gaze on Him; to open our hearts, minds and souls to Him, and receive the inflow of Spirit-life to restore harassed and burdened souls. But we were not designed to be its slaves. Sabbath is given to serve us with the riches of restoration

'Sabbath... is a gift'

that we need to fulfil our potential in our God-given 'promised-land life' and enjoy His promised blessings.

A gift not a burden

'The Sabbath was made for man, not man for the Sabbath.' (**Mark 2:27**)

Obviously, there is no one-size-fits-all type of Sabbath. My daughter is 'Mummy' to three young boys who demand her care and attention seven days of the week. I have a friend with twins; one of whom is incredibly bright needing constant stimulation, the other who is severely handicapped in both body and brain: unable to see, to eat solid food or turn over unaided in bed. I also know people who are full-time carers for a dependent spouse or parent. So Sabbath should not condemn us, but inspire us to reach out for God's gift in ways that are appropriate to our own situation, especially where there are genuine reasons (as opposed to excuses) why taking a day out to rest with God is impossible.

Some women arrange child or parent care to create two hours each week alone in God's Word, while others take mini Sabbaths each day, when time allows, to sit still, breathe deeply, and intentionally turn their heart and mind on God with them. So be creative! Explore ideas with a friend or church leader. Know that God accepts your limitations, but longs to restore the inflow of His Spirit-life rest within them. And for those of us tempted to make an excuse not to have a Sabbath (though we should be able to), let's embrace this command for the loving,

God-given gift that it is, and its importance in restoring the balance of God's fullness with our lives in the world. The three key phrases of this command are:

'Remember the Sabbath day' (Exod. 20:8). In other words, if you keep forgetting to spend time with God, or allow inappropriate intrusions to invade it, then put it in your diary. Try and make sure some time each week is scheduled for God. This need not necessarily be a Saturday or Sunday but whenever suits your routine.

'by keeping it holy' (v8). A sabbath rest is a day to be especially present with God in mind and heart; not with a stiff, religious, one-eye-on-the-clock, 'ought-to' mentality, but taking pleasure in whatever enables you to focus more intently on who He is to you. A day to honour and love Him, rest in and appreciate His world with Him. Taking time to read Scripture and to pray is essential to opening your heart to the inflow of God's Spirit-life, but Sabbath isn't

> 'time with God… to focus on His love, faithfulness, power and provision.'

all about study and intercession. It's about worship, dependency, and absorbing God's truth. It's about having time with God with no agenda other than to focus on His love, faithfulness, power and provision. Sabbath rest also comes from enjoying God's good gifts: creation, homes, families, friends and hobbies. It's simply about letting God be whatever He chooses to be to you in that moment.

'On it you shall not do any work' (v10). A Sabbath is time to enjoy God. To 'enjoy' implies taking pleasure in Him and how He created you, without the demands of work. Work might not

necessarily mean paid employment – many people work long hours for little or no pay. Generally speaking though, work is whatever God has called you to do for six days a week to further His kingdom; the outflow of His Spirit-life through you. The meaning of 'work' in this verse will be your regular activity that you need to pause from in order to have some time of spiritual refreshing with Jesus; time away from deadlines, projects, pressures, serving, and giving out.

What constitutes work differs from person to person. Although my work during the week is as a writer and speaker, Sunday couldn't be my Sabbath because I am part of my church leadership team. However, Sunday for you might be the one day you can shut down the computer, hide the vacuum cleaner, switch off the phone – and just 'be'.

So when you're wondering what to do on your Sabbath, the question to ask is: 'Will this activity deplete or re-energise me?' I've read many articles about the Sabbath, which suggest having a 'special' meal with family ('special' usually implying something more than boiled eggs). This idea works if the person who's going to prep, cook and serve that 'special' meal is someone who wouldn't get frazzled, but would find rest, refreshment and would relish time out with God in the kitchen. A person who would see it as an opportunity to thank Him for the food being chopped, to pray for those who will enjoy it, and to maybe even sing worship songs while stirring simmering pots. (That person certainly isn't me!)

It is a good idea to reflect on what you might be tempted to do on your Sabbath that drains you rather than restores you. Rather than keep digging the hard-packed soil of your God-given 'promised land', lie down for a while in His green pastures

(Psa. 23:2), and remember how God made you, provided for you, and wants to restore the balance of His Spirit-life in you.

Jesus said, 'Come to me… and I will give you rest' (Matt. 11:28) and to His disciples after a busy period, 'Come with me by yourselves to a quiet place and get some rest' (Mark 6:31). As disciples of Jesus, we are called to be with Him, and to be sent out by Him. We are called to be yoked with Jesus, living and working in harmonious partnership with Him but we are also called to Sabbath; a place of comfort, release, restoration and empowering.

As we end this section on 'being with Jesus' and start another on 'being sent out', let's not lose sight of how 'being with Jesus' includes resting with Him, and is essential to our subsequent fruitfulness for His kingdom.

Getting personal – making this real

> *'Sabbath is God's metronome, marking out a weekly rhythm of rest and renewal. It is our reference point for knowing how to plan and live our lives. Without the Sabbath, our lives are a jumbled mess of individual events; with Sabbath, they can be a beautiful balance of labor and rest… Unless God's rhythm of rest sets the baseline beat, we will miss the composer's intent for our lives – and His intent is shalom.'* Kerri Weems[15]

— **What day would work best for *your* Sabbath each week? If you needed to be flexible, what other day would make a good alternative? Get your diary and mark those days as 'Sabbath' as far ahead as you can.**

— What environment would ensure rest for your body, mind, emotions and spirit? For example, would turning off technology or social media, getting away from home, or staying at home help you step off your treadmill?

— What are the 'quiet waters' (Psa. 23:2) that invite you to drink deeply of God in His Word and prayer? To love and be loved? To delight and be delighted in? To know and be known? To be taught and to listen? Whatever your need, I pray that you may know that even the sighs of your heart are heard and understood by your Father.

— What do you currently do on your Sabbath that saps its potential for rest, peace, joy, restoration and positivity? Reflect on whether these activities are really important to your kingdom life and responsibilities? Remember that God has called you to a rhythm of work and rest. If they are not so relevant, then get rid of them, stop pursuing them, let them go – at least, until another season of life.

Saying 'yes' to any and all requests that come your way, and finding yourself having to fulfil those responsibilities on the day intended for Sabbath, is a sure route to burnout. Be confident in who you are in God, and to what He has and has not called you to do.

— What activities would you like to introduce to your Sabbath that will give you God-given pleasure;

for example, a coffee with a friend, a long walk or reading?

Give yourself permission to acknowledge the way God made you, and He knows the pleasures that will restore your soul without diverting your attention from being in His presence.

Lord, I come to You now with my thoughts, emotions, longings and hurts. Take this burden I'm trying to carry alone [name it and talk to God about it]. Help me to be still. To be quiet. To rest in a place of cessation from the struggles and battles of working the 'promised land'. To see, and feel, life from Your perspective, and may my 'promised-land life' be a place of deep inexpressible calm and self-assurance. Amen.

Part Three

RESTORING THE OUTFLOW

Restoring the outflow —
introducing the theme

'continue to work out your salvation with fear and trembling, for it is God who works in you to will and to act in order to fulfil his good purpose.' **(Phil. 2:12–13)**

Beginning at the foot of Mount Hermon in the north of Israel, the River Jordan is the longest and most important river in the Promised Land, geographically dividing west from east as it gains momentum heading south. Its essential life-giving waters irrigate crops, and sustain the health of flocks, herds and tribes. The river's long journey is halted, however, when it plunges into the deepest lake in the world: the landlocked Dead Sea, immersed in the low-lying barren Judean desert. Without any water outlet, a rapid evaporation occurs in the intense desert heat, depositing vast quantities of salt: sparkling white encrusted shores lacing it's cobalt beauty, which glitters silver or gold in the morning or evening light. But as attractive as it appears, those once life-giving waters can no longer sustain even macroscopic life-forms.

The Dead Sea is a sobering visual aid when we think about nurturing our own 'promised-land life'; if we're being 'fed and filled' from Sunday church, mid-week groups and our personal devotions, but never passing it on, we may lose our spiritual vitality as it stagnates then ceases to be a source of God's life to others. And in turn God's Spirit-life in us is skewed out of balance with our life in the world.

Do you believe God is working in you to fulfil His purposes?

While interviewing Eugene Peterson, Sheridan Voysey asked him how he ordered his spiritual life: what disciplines and practices he used to maintain his relationship with God. Peterson replied: 'To tell you the truth, Sheridan, I don't really think of that time as devotional time. I'm praying, I'm reading the Bible, I'm meditating; I'm just trying to be present before God. But when I leave my study, that's when I begin. I feel like [that morning time] is the stretching and callisthenics you do before you run a race. Then you're into the world and you're praying. That's when the praying starts—grappling with life in Jesus' name.'[16]

This perfectly sums up the purpose of this book: to inspire you to connect and be open to the inflow of God's Spirit-life, and to daily walk in the awareness of His presence with you. To put it another way, how to live your physical tangible life in ongoing harmony with God's Spirit-life flowing through you.

'daily walk in the awareness of His presence with you.'

We don't work to earn our salvation; it's a gift of grace freely given to all and received by faith. However, we are to be intentional in expressing its reality as an ongoing process of our spiritual growth and maturity. The phrase 'work out our salvation' (Phil. 2:12) means put into practice what God has worked in us by His Spirit. So let's willingly do what He has asked us to do while being in constant dependence on Him. Whether it's roles we fulfil in our family, church, in paid or voluntary employment, the influential outflow of God's ongoing work relies on His enabling plus our willingness to do as He asks: co-labourers with Him in kingdom work on earth.

> 'Let's willingly do what He has asked us to do'

This spiritual dependency won't always feel natural, at least not when we're busy with the mundane, enjoying the good times, or getting on with the many things we feel capable of doing. Seeking to serve God, however, is about the 'supernatural' equipping the 'natural'; to lace and grace our natural life with the 'super-natural' Spirit-life of God.

Paul writes: 'we have this treasure in jars of clay to show that this all-surpassing power is from God and not from us' (2 Cor. 4:7), or, as Mike Pilavachi helpfully translates, 'God puts his treasure in our jars of clay, and the life seeps out through the cracks!'[17] We have the extraordinary power of heaven ready to flow in and out of our ordinary lives, and without it, we 'can do nothing' (John 15:5) of kingdom significance.

Getting personal – making this real

'Remember what you are saved for—that the Son of God might be manifested in your mortal flesh. Bend the whole energy of your powers to realise your election as a child of God; rise to the occasion every time. You cannot do anything for your salvation, but you must do something to manifest it, you must work out what God has worked in… we are not here to dictate to God; we are here to submit to His will so that He may work though us what He wants. When we realise this, He will make us broken bread and poured-out wine to feed and nourish others.' Oswald Chambers[18]

'Be energetic in your life of salvation, reverent and sensitive before God. That energy is God's *energy, an energy deep within you, God himself willing and working at what will give him the most pleasure.'*
(**Phil. 2:13,** *The Message*)

— **What energises you? In what ways do you sense God wanting to work through you, and will you be open to that?**

'I can do all this through him who give me strength.'
(**Phil. 4:13**)

— **What might be the 'all this' or work that God is calling you to do for Him?**

— **What is preventing you from carrying out this work? What steps might be needed to put yourself in the place He wants you to be? Remember that God will be with you and working through you to fulfil His purpose.**

— **Jesus teaches us to 'seek first his kingdom and his righteousness' (Matt. 6:33) because any other goal is meaningless from the perspective of eternal life and holds back the outflow of God's Spirit-life in you. Who are you seeking to please? Or what are you seeking to achieve? How are you going about doing those things?**

Jesus was perfectly focused on His Father's will. Sometimes we might strive to achieve something that is beyond our abilities, and it can distract us from our true purpose. But Jesus said: 'Let anyone who is thirsty come to me and drink. Whoever believes in me, as Scripture has said, rivers of living water will flow from within them' (John 7:37–38). This is an awesome promise, which helps us put our confidence in God and in who He made us to be. Let's be encouraged by the life-giving impact of His divine anointing, which releases us to fulfil the best of our God-given potential in the 'promised-land life' He has called us to work.

The outflow doesn't just happen by reading, hearing, or even believing God's Word; faith needs to be expressed in action. We can pray something, say something, or do something in order that the awesome power of God's presence flows through us. For the rest of this section, we will be looking at examples of how we can encourage a greater outflow of God's Spirit-life to influence others and impact the world with His kingdom.

God of peace, please equip me with good things to do Your will, and work in me what is pleasing to You, through Jesus Christ, to whom be glory for ever and ever. Amen.

Restoring the outflow —
through agape *love*

"'Of all the commandments, which is the
most important?' "The most important one,"
answered Jesus, "is this: 'Hear, O Israel: the
Lord our God, the Lord is one. Love the
Lord your God with all your heart and with
all your soul and with all your mind and
with all your strength.' The second is this:
'Love your neighbour as yourself.' There
is no commandment greater than these.'"
(**Mark 12:28–31**)

Lord, I do believe You love all people equally, but sometimes
I struggle to treat difficult, irritating, unreliable, unkind or
demeaning people with the same love I treat my closest friends and
loved ones. Help me look beyond my own needs and step outside my
natural responses to restore the outflow of Your agape *love. Amen.*

I had held her in awe for some years: savouring every word of her
books and articles; nourished and challenged by her Bible study
notes. So excitement mounted as I drove to a writers' conference
where she would be the keynote speaker, lead a seminar *and*
offer one-to-ones. That's where I first met one of my heroines
of the faith – Jennifer Rees Larcombe. She was amazing; witty
yet gracious; warm yet authoritative; kind, gentle and a font of

wisdom on all things 'writing', so I signed up for a one-to-one. A while later, I was invited to her home to talk further, which was later followed up by a request to be part of her *Beauty from Ashes*[19] ministry team.

From the moment I sat down for a one-to-one with Jennifer, I felt special, loved, appreciated and of value to someone who barely even knew me. This friendship helped me to grow in confidence in who I was in God; His healing love working deep within my soul, and shedding light on wounds still raw but buried in the darkness of getting on and coping with 'today'.

However, I soon learned a vital lesson: Jennifer treated everyone like that – the other members of her team, the people who maintained her beautiful garden, her administration staff and trustees, and everyone who walked through the door of her home, the door of a conference or retreat centre; in fact, everyone who walked through the door of her life. Everyone she met was loved, welcomed, wanted, valued, listened to, understood, cared for, appreciated and significant. During the years I served alongside her, I repeatedly and consistently saw the fullness of God's love flowing out to all she met, even to those who tested her kindness, patience and grace, and even when she was wearied by intense ministry schedules and painful health problems.

Jennifer's life showed me *agape* love in action. *Agape* is the ancient Greek word used in the Bible to describe the way God loves. We naturally feel *phileo* love: a personal attachment and affection for close friends or family. To experience the unmerited love of God, however, and to deliberately reflect that love to others is not easy when someone irritates us, aggressively argues their viewpoint, is brash, disrespectful and arrogant, rejects our beliefs, chooses a lifestyle that jars with our own, or who has caused us deep hurt.

Seeing people from God's perspective

As the inflow of God's Spirit-life sheds light on our inner being, it helps us to see people as He does. Our eyes and ears may see or hear degrading habits, offensive words, ungodly conduct and rebellious attitudes. God, however, wants us to look beyond what we can see with our eyes and perceive a person's fear, neediness and insecurity; to respect and care for those who may have good reasons for why they act, respond or struggle with life as they do. When we look at a person through the lens of God's love, we remember they are created in His image. The selfishness, greed, problems and pain of their broken world may mask His glory, but it is there in seed form. Regardless of who they are or what they have done, every person should be treated with love, respect, dignity, care and attention. This doesn't mean that we shouldn't, where necessary, set appropriate boundaries, implement safety measures, or draw attention to unhelpful behaviour because we are all accountable for our actions no matter what our background. Fundamentally though, God's Spirit-life calls us to love unreservedly and without judgment.

> 'When we look at a person through the lens of God's love, we remember they are created in His image'

To choose to see people as God does helps us to be fully present when talking to others, and to focus our minds, hearts, spirits and emotions on what they are sharing. If we're worried about our workload or the time of our next appointment, distracted by our own problems or thinking about our response while they're still speaking, we are not being truly present. To be present is to listen, and not just to hear. It is to focus without distraction. It is to empathise. By showing Christlike love, we give space for God's Spirit-life to help us see the person as He does; to help us discern what to say or do; or to receive a word of knowledge for their situation.

God is described as bringing us into a 'spacious place' (Psa. 18:19) – a safe, peaceful place to flourish and experience worth, hope and joy. When we choose to see people as God does, and let His love shape our words and responses, it helps them experience that same wonderful 'spacious place' of God in us.

Biblical examples of how God sees people

In her distress and vulnerability as a pregnant slave woman, fleeing alone through potentially hostile territory, Hagar experienced the love and care of God. In her moment of need, Hagar realised she was known by God who cared for her wellbeing, saying, 'You are the God who sees me' (Gen. 16:13). God asked her about her past and where she was heading. He saw the danger of her exposed position. He responded with the wisdom she needed that would place her back in the protection of a community and give her hope for the safety of her child.

Returning to the camp of her bitter mistress would not have been easy, but Hagar was comforted knowing God was with her, and had placed her in the best situation available for both herself and her unborn child – for that period of time at least.

God doesn't just see, He looks out for *all* people, and we are called to look out for them too. Regardless of their nationality, ethnicity, accent, cultural habits, religion, lifestyle, personal hygiene, choice of clothing, vivid tattoos, number and location of body piercings, style or colour of hair, we are to let the fullness of God's love for us ripple out to others that they may *know* God loves and cares for them too.

'Then [Jesus] turned toward the woman and said to Simon, "Do you see this woman?"' (Luke 7:44). Simon could not help but see the woman to whom Jesus was referring – she was a prostitute. Uninvited and unwelcome as a guest in his home, she was acting inappropriately: weeping over Jesus' feet, drying off smutty tears with her hair, kissing and smearing them with her vulgar fragrance, which was no doubt bought from her dubious 'business' profits. Simon could see the person in front of him, but he didn't look for any truth behind the appearance or for how God might be at work in her life.

Jesus saw her differently. Perhaps He saw a background that had led her to believe she was undeserving of a man's love and care; experiences of rejection and abandonment, which left her with little choice as to how to earn a living in a culture devoid of social benefits, and where women relied on a husband's financial support; or maybe she'd made some very poor choices with her life. We don't know why she turned to prostitution, but Jesus did, and He also saw past it to the heart of a woman who had evidently seen Him show mercy to others; a woman who could not help but love Jesus because He lavished love on everyone whether rich or poor. Jesus saw a woman who was desperate for the forgiveness and new start in life that she'd heard Him teach about; a woman driven to grasp an opportunity to get close to Him in a place unhampered by the crowds. Slipping in uninvited, she poured out her love by washing and anointing His feet: symbols of hospitality that Simon had neglected to perform.

God may or may not give us words of knowledge about certain aspects of a person's life, but we can still learn to 'see' them as He does, as we look past the outward appearance and let God's Spirit-life flow out with love for their immense worth to Him.

In Psalms we read: 'The LORD is close to the brokenhearted and saves those who are crushed in spirit… A father to the fatherless, a defender of widows, is God in his holy dwelling. God sets the lonely in families' (Psa. 34:18; 68:5–6). God's heart is to draw close to the brokenhearted, destitute, impoverished, poor, refugee, and the physically, mentally or emotionally broken, and to do that through us. This might mean we need to get out of our usual comfort zone in order to be in a place to hear their cry, and be willing to get our hands, face and clothes dirty as we help them. We may need to make time to stop and listen, to feel their pain, and to offer enduring friendship. We may need to grow godly patience when we hear their story repeated time and again, simply because there are rarely quick-fix solutions.

> 'God's heart is to draw close to the brokenhearted… through us.'

It's easy to pop briefly into someone's life then walk straight back out again, but it takes selfless giving to walk their journey, help them to have a voice and be their defence. We need to choose to unblock any prejudice or hindrance and let God's Spirit-life love flow through us.

Restoring the outflow of God's agape love

Jesus showed us how God extends and conveys His love to everyone, and we are to convey that love to our world, whether or not it is reciprocated. Jesus ate and socialised with the ungodly; He did not condemn the woman caught in adultery but encouraged her to change her way of life; and He restored the reputation of Zacchaeus who felt he had let God down. Jesus was compassionate, sympathetic, empathetic and understanding. He felt, and was moved by, human pain. He wasn't afraid to touch the ostracised and isolated, to welcome the uninvited, and serve His oppressors. He welcomed both young and old, and conveyed His message of forgiveness to those who abused Him so terribly. Crucially, He pursued people estranged from God, rather than spending all His time with believers.

While Jesus gave generously of Himself, He also knew how to care for Himself; He wasn't available 24/7, and nor did He expect His disciples to be. There are many examples of Jesus taking Himself off alone to pray, of going on to another village when the crowd urged Him to stay, and of taking His disciples away to a quiet place to rest.

Loving others as Jesus does means loving ourselves enough to care for our own needs too. Unless we love ourselves – that is, take care of our emotional, spiritual, mental and physical wellbeing – we will have nothing to give out, and will potentially put our own health at risk.

Getting personal – making this real

'Agape *moved heaven to earth in mighty force, and* agape *lifts earth to heaven in transforming power.* Agape *sent God to man and ever since has raised man to God. No wonder it is the greatest, and no doubt it is the grandest, experience of Spirit life.'* Stuart Briscoe[20]

Commit to rereading the Gospel accounts of Jesus, and as you do, picture and reflect on how Jesus 'perfectly mirrors God, is stamped with God's nature' (Heb. 1:3, *The Message*).

— **Are there some people that you find difficult to love? What is it about them that frustrates, annoys, hurts or undermines you? Prayerfully mull on how you might respond in the power of God's Spirit-life in future, and ask God to help you see them as He does.**
— **What boundaries might you need to set in place to protect your spiritual health?**
— **How can you encourage others to help you love and shoulder the needs of your family and friends?**

All-loving, all-seeing Father of my heart, help me to see as You see, to love as You love, and choose to respond to people just as You do to me. Amen.

Restoring the outflow —
through witness

'Therefore go and make disciples of all nations, baptising them in the name of the Father and of the Son and of the Holy Spirit'
(**Matt. 28:19**)

Lord, I believe in Your longing for all men to be saved, and that You've called me to partner Your kingdom work by sharing Your truth with others. But I'm just too timid; I've been put off by failed attempts to share my faith in the past, and, if I'm honest, most times I don't even think about it. Help me to be a channel for the flow of Your heart to reach lost souls. Amen.

'GO!' That one word from Matthew 28:19 was printed across our Youth With a Mission t-shirts as we set out from the campus for a two-month mission to India. Eager and expectant that God would perform miraculous works, we laid hands on the deaf, blind and sick. Fuelled by a gregarious faith, we stopped strangers with the name of Jesus on our lips.

'Go!' reflected four months' training based on Christ's command to make disciples of all nations; a passage often proclaimed in rousing sermons or used to commission missionaries. But although I was open for God to send me anywhere in the world, at the end of the mission and debrief, He sent me straight back home.

Paul writes: 'make it your ambition' – your daily goal – 'to lead a quiet life: you should mind your own business and work with your hands… so that your daily life' – your daily, humdrum, ever so normal 24 hour routine – 'may win the respect of outsiders' (1 Thess. 4:11–12). Jesus didn't just say 'Go, make disciples' to the short- or long-term missionaries, to the evangelists or church leaders. God has a heart and purpose for those who stay at home as well as for those who change their roles, homes, or even their country in obedience to His command to share His truth with others.

We might feel that we're not gifted evangelists, or be afraid of ridicule or rejection, but by making these excuses we hold back the outflow of God's Spirit-life; something that can also occur if we become so preoccupied with serving the saved that we've no time or interest for the unsaved souls still lost outside church walls, or if we're so immersed in this physical life that our heart no longer beats in time with God's heart for the lost. So 'staying' doesn't nullify His directive to make disciples, it just means we 'Go!' and do it in the world on our own doorstep.

Restoring the outflow of Spirit empowered witness

People. People are the target recipients for the gospel message of God's kingdom. Jesus didn't die for our work, our homes, our possessions or our church agendas, but for people – for you, me and everyone else to know, and receive, His gift of eternal life. 'God our Saviour… wants all people to be saved and to come to a knowledge of the truth' (1 Tim. 2:3–4).

People. We can't take anything else from this world into our life with God but people. If we are going to invest our time and energy into anything, then let it be in people: loving them, caring for them, supporting them, teaching them, listening to them, embracing them and seeking to understand them.

'If we are going to invest our time and energy into anything, then let it be in people'

People are at the heart of God's Spirit-life flowing into us, and therefore at the heart of His kingdom life flowing out, but I wonder to what extent that our desires, goals and use of resources are focused on things other than people.

God anoints some of us with the spiritual gift of evangelism, which I've heard described as someone who is gifted like a lawyer to present a case in a court of law with convincing facts and arguments. I'm not a spiritually gifted evangelist, and perhaps you aren't either, but God has called *all* of us to be witnesses, to simply share what we've experienced, seen, heard, read and know to be true.

The jury is watching and listening to us – a jury made up of our friends, family, colleagues and those we reach out to practically with God's love. We have been sent into their world as the bridge between the reality of God and their doubts, indecision or lack of faith. Whether they choose to walk across the bridge to meet with God personally is their choice; our responsibility is to make clear who He is.

Let's explore three ways that we can be a Spirit-filled witness to others.

1. Live a life of endless praise

'Walk the talk!' 'Practise what you preach!' Just two familiar catchphrases that suggest our lives are often the only 'sermon' some people will ever be faced with; a message that shows, rather than tells, what being 'in Christ' implies for day-to-day life and responses.

Paul teaches us to live lives 'for the praise of [God's] glory' (Eph. 1:12); to have attitudes and behaviour that turn people's attention onto God's truth and grace. We are to shine like stars in the godless environments we might find ourselves. As *The Message* puts it: 'Go out into the world uncorrupted, a breath of fresh air in this squalid and polluted society. Provide people with a glimpse of good living and of the living God. Carry the light-giving Message into the night' (Phil. 2:15–16).

We can't sing praise songs 24 hours a day every day but our lives can be vessels of endless praise. Our joy, zeal and trust in the fullness of God's character can be a visible outflow of devotion and gratitude, affirming what we say about the God in who we believe.

Alternatively, we can thwart the outflow of our witness, and dissuade others from having any interest in Him. Instead of having the assured, quiet confidence that comes from trusting a faithful God who promises to be with us in every situation, we are beset by worry, insecurity and fear, which suggest to the onlooker that God is not as dependable as we say. Instead of letting God's love and character flow out through us, we let natural reactions override His Spirit-life responses, which dissuades others from wanting to get to know Him for themselves. Instead of having joy and contentment intrinsic to being in Christ, we grumble, complain or criticise, which implies that there might be more hope for happiness by looking for it in the world than being in relationship with God.

We all encounter problems, suffering and grief, but as we depend on God's strength, comfort and provision, our godly perspective will impact those who are blinkered by world boundaries.

2. Build bridges

In the many homes we've lived, my husband and I have been fortunate to get on well with our neighbours, which have included atheists, agnostics and spiritualists. We enjoy chatting over the fence, sharing meals in each other's homes, or connecting with each other at local events, but neither of us are spiritually gifted evangelists, so the challenge is: how do we bridge God's Spirit-life in us with His absence in theirs?

It takes effort to sow seeds and then patiently wait for the harvest. Earning the right to speak spiritual truth into someone's life takes an investment of time, love, kindness, wisdom, loyalty and grace. Sometimes an opportunity to share testimony and the gospel is immediate, but sometimes it can take far longer – time that can be well used to build bridges of friendship and trust as we 'walk the talk' and prepare to answer questions that arise. Every interaction, every conversation, every kindness is an opportunity to share Jesus. However, time is short for their choice to be made, and we may be the only person offering God's gift. So as soon as we're prompted to go deeper, let's not hold back from taking the next step to engage them with the truth.

3. Be intentional (but sensitive) about sharing your faith

Peter writes, 'Always be prepared to give an answer to everyone who asks you to give the reason for the hope that you have. But do this with gentleness and respect' (1 Pet. 3:15). That's not an easy thing to do for some of us, so here are some ideas that might help:

- **Look for ways to elevate conversation from the mundane to more meaningful themes.** You can develop this skill as you learn to listen well to someone. Be present and undistracted in the moment with them. Listening with an open heart to God's Spirit helps inspire the deeper questions; a passing comment may actually be rich with potential if you pick up any hint that it could lead on to something more profound.

- **Be confident in your testimony and how you might share it, should the opportunity present itself.** Write down how meeting God has helped you and then refine it so it is clear, concise and engaging. Remind yourself of it often so that you will always be prepared when someone asks you what brought you to faith.

- **Learn how to explain the gospel simply.** There are plenty of ideas online or in books but choose one that suits your personality, then make it your own so that it doesn't just sound like a regurgitated script. Cultural relevancy, a personal story and humour will help engage your listener, much like the way Jesus shared truth through parables.

  When I was new to the faith, my beliefs took a battering by those who opposed Christianity and whose arguments I couldn't respond to. Thirty-five years later and those same questions are still being bandied about, such as: 'Why does a God of love allow suffering?' 'Who was Jesus?' 'What makes you believe in the resurrection?' 'Why are there apparent discrepancies in the Bible?' There are plenty of books, blogs, podcasts and even conferences that address apologetics for those of us not gifted to be an apologist ourselves. Ask your leaders at church to help you understand and engage with some of these issues, which will hopefully grow your confidence to share your faith.

Faith implies there will always be something of the higher ways and thoughts of God that we cannot understand – otherwise He would not be God! But the more we know, the more relaxed we will be when faced with opportunities to share; more confident in what and who we know, but filled with God's gracious Spirit-life of gentleness and respect.

- **Ask God for opportunities.** Keep your eyes and heart open to people who cross your path each day, and be God's kingdom ambassador.

- **Identify your 'frontline'.** Paul was sent to the Gentiles, Peter to the Jews. Who has God sent you to? In June 2018, social media widely acclaimed Chris Pratt as one of the greatest evangelists of

> 'Keep your eyes and heart open to people who cross your path each day, and be God's kingdom ambassador.'

our time in response to his acceptance speech for an MTV award where he spoke in an engaging and relevant way to young people. I enjoyed watching his speech and gained some valuable tips, but was also challenged to apply what I learned, even though my frontline is so very different.

It a good idea to spend some time reflecting on your own frontline and who is in your sphere of influence; perhaps your work colleagues, your neighbours or your children. Think about what your friends are interested in as well as who, or what, preoccupies them. Ask God, by the outflow of His Spirit-life in you, to enable you to speak into their lives in a language they will relate to.

I am challenged by this verse: 'Therefore, I declare to you today that I am innocent of the blood of any of you. For I have not hesitated to proclaim to you the whole will of God' (Acts 20:26–27). Would I be 'innocent of the blood' of people in my world who don't love God? Have I allowed God's love and truth in me to flow out and reach out to them? I cannot be responsible for their choice, but I am responsible for ensuring they know that there *is* a choice on offer and that it needs to be made.

Getting personal – making this real

'Your ministry is your service to believers, and your mission is your service to unbelievers… it's more important than any job, achievement, or goal you will reach during your life on earth… The eternal salvation of a single soul is more important than anything else you will ever achieve in life. Only people are going to last forever.' Rick Warren[21]

Jesus' command to share the good news and make disciples is often given the title 'The Great Commission', but it is not 'The Greatest Commandment', which is to love God, and subsequently love our neighbour.

— **What encourages you to share your belief? Is it love for the other person, or are you just out to 'win' the faith debate?**

Look again at people from God's perspective. See how He loves them, and how His love, together with the magnetic draw of Jesus, might aid your further witness.

— **Although we are citizens of heaven, we live in this world as 'Christ's ambassadors' (2 Cor. 5:20). We act and speak as if Jesus were present Himself. How do your words and lifestyle reflect the culture of heaven?**
— **To whom have you been sent to convey messages from your King?**
— **How is God specifically inspiring or challenging you through your answers to these questions?**

Never underestimate the power of Spirit-filled prayer. Write a list of the names of your friends, family and colleagues who don't yet know God personally. Place it somewhere obvious where you'll be prompted to pray intentionally for each one, and for a breakthrough in the spiritual realm over all that holds them back and blinds them to truth.

Lord, please open my eyes that I may make the most of every opportunity to let Your Spirit-life confirm Your truth to others. Show me how I can be all things to all people, entering their world to understand it, so that by all possible means You might work through me to save some. Amen.

Restoring the outflow — *through* charismata

'For just as each of us has one body with many members, and these members do not all have the same function, so in Christ we, though many, form one body, and each member belongs to all the others. We have different gifts, according to the grace given to each of us.' (**Rom. 12:4–6**)

Lord, I do believe I am a part of Your body, the church, and that You want to anoint and enable me to fulfil my role. But I hesitate to step up to it, afraid You might not equip me in the moment of need, afraid of what people will think or say, afraid of making mistakes, and afraid of committing yet more time that I don't feel I have, or that I want to reserve for other things. Help me overcome any barriers to my letting You anoint me for the part you have chosen for me to fulfil. Amen.

When I applied for my Youth With A Mission course, I was willing for God to send me anywhere to do whatever He wanted through my life. I was completely open for God to transform timid me into a zealous full-time missionary, if that was His desire. Throughout my trip, however, the missionary idea never once resonated with how God was stirring my heart. What *did* resonate, and I have to say unexpectedly, was the pleasure and inspiration that came from recording each day in my journal: meticulously wordsmithing life-changing experiences, and all that God was teaching me in His Word. It took some years, however, before I recognised that experience as God igniting His anointing on me to write.

Similarly, we had been trained and encouraged to go out onto the streets and claim healing in Jesus' name. Much to my amazement, a few folk *were* healed of blindness and deafness as I prayed, but I couldn't help noticing how some members of the team were particularly being used by God to heal people. My team leader, for example, prayed for someone with a disfigured leg and, as I watched, the leg stretched out, took on shape and form and the person was healed. For some time afterwards, it left me thinking I'd failed; that my faith was inadequate to please God or hadn't been strong enough to pray for as many healings as my friends. I've since realised, however, that God hadn't gifted me specifically with a healing ministry (which, I must say, restored my peace). I've also looked back and remembered how my leaders would often ask me to share a team devotional thought, or to give a short talk in local churches; leaders who had evidently discerned (as others have since, and long before I ever did) God's anointing on my life to teach His Word.

Every part of a body works alongside the other parts, to ensure the whole body functions properly. Likewise, you and I are filled by the Holy Spirit to be Christ's body in the world today; each of us spiritually empowered to perform different parts of His ministry, but working *together* to ensure His work

'God has not equipped one person to do everything.'

continues in all its fullness. God has not equipped one person to do everything. The body is weakened when some of its members refuse to play their part, holding back the outflow of God's Spirit-life to others, but team work – body ministry – is the outflow of God's Spirit-life through His Church.

Charismata or spiritual gifts

Charismata is the ancient Greek word used in the Bible to mean 'spiritual gifts': the free, unmerited manifestation of God's power and enabling. A number of passages in the Bible suggest how spiritual gifts can be manifested, but these descriptions and lists are by no means exhaustive. The enabling of the Holy Spirit goes beyond the limits of what can be included in Scripture.

Psalm 139 talks of a divine knowingness when we were knit together in our mother's womb; of God-created natural talents to be nurtured through opportunity, or trial and error in life. Sometimes our natural talents help us to discern God's purpose and calling for us, though not always. Sometimes they may help us convey His truth, for example, through music or art. Sometimes, again not always, they dovetail with the way He determines to anoint us with spiritual gifts (for example, a teacher who comes to faith and is then anointed to preach).

Charismata don't always have an obvious link to our natural gifts. Spiritual gifts depend on God's spiritual anointing. When seeking to receive spiritual gifts and so restore the outflow of God's Spirit through our lives into the world, it is helpful to reflect on the following points:

Desire it

'Follow the way of love and eagerly desire spiritual gifts,
especially prophecy' (**1 Cor. 14:1**).

Jesus modelled a life lived in the flesh that was in perfect balance
with a life filled with God's Spirit – a life we can experience in
increasing measure if that is our desire. The Holy Spirit doesn't
force Himself on us, because to do so would contradict His
loving, gentle and considerate nature – besides, God has given
us freedom of choice. He does, however, long that we would
desire His abundant Spirit-life in full measure. He wants us
to experience the spiritual life He intended, even though our
physical life is still marred by the fallen world. Let's take care not
to 'put out' the Spirit's fire by not desiring and asking for it due to
a disinterested, apathetic or cynical attitude.

I find that praying my own adaptation of Ephesians 3:16–21
(see the prayer at end of this chapter) stirs this longing within me,
and because I am praying God's Word, my heart is expectant to
receive what I have asked.

Remember who this is about

'for it is God who works in you to will and to act in order to
fulfill his good purpose' (**Phil. 2:13**).

John the Baptist said of Jesus, 'He must become greater; I must
become less' (John 3:30). John knew his fruitful ministry in the
desert had to draw to a close in order to draw people's attention
to Jesus' ministry.

The 'I' in us must step aside to let God's Spirit-life fill us to full measure with His awesome equipping and empowering. This is God's work, so God will strengthen us with whatever we need to achieve it. We need not be afraid of not being capable when we pursue His purpose and calling.

> 'The 'I' in us must step aside to let God's Spirit-life fill us to full measure with His awesome equipping and empowering.'

Surrender to God's will

> *'All these are the work of one and the same Spirit, and he distributes them to each one, just as he determines'*
>
> **(1 Cor. 12:11)**.

God chooses how He will equip us with *charismata*. That's not our decision, but if we persistently resist because we're not willing to be used, or because we want Him to use us differently, it will limit His anointing from flowing out in full measure. God's Spirit-life enabling is rooted in love; its very purpose is to build up and enrich others with the life of Jesus, and enhance our witness. With love, there is no place for competition or pride, and every part of the body is needed to function as God intended.

God's Spirit dwelt fully, perfectly and consistently in Jesus in order to express His character and minister in His power. All of us now share the ongoing ministry of His body; a body of many parts all working together in harmony. We can't all be or do the same thing, or the rest of the body will fail to function to its full potential.

Getting personal – making this real

'If the Holy Spirit was withdrawn from the church today, 95% of what we do would go on and no one would know the difference. If the Holy Spirit had been withdrawn from the New Testament church, 95% of what they did would stop, and everybody would know the difference.' A.W. Tozer[22]

Whenever I read this quote by A.W. Tozer I catch myself nodding, with a wry smile teasing my lips as my thoughts turn to the Church in general. Moments later, I'm convicted and think: 'Hang on, I'm part of the Church, so what about me? Am *I* living my day-to-day life depending on God's empowering?'

— **Are you daily depending out God's empowering?**

'There are different kinds of gifts, but the same Spirit distributes them. There are different kinds of service, but the same Lord. There are different kinds of working, but in all of them and in everyone it is the same God at work. Now to each one the manifestation of the Spirit is given for the common good' (**1 Cor. 12:4–7**).

— **Asking for more of God's Spirit-life anointing and empowering is admirable, but are you truly willing and available, to let God work through you how He chooses? Or would you prefer that He anoint you in the way *you* want Him to?**

> '*In those days when the number of disciples was increasing, the Hellenistic Jews among them complained against the Hebraic Jews because their widows were being overlooked in the daily distribution of food. So the Twelve gathered all the disciples together and said, "It would not be right for us to neglect the ministry of the word of God in order to wait on tables. Brothers and sisters, choose seven men from among you who are known to be full of the Spirit and wisdom. We will turn this responsibility over to them and will give our attention to prayer and the ministry of the word"*' (**Acts 6:1–4**).

You might feel that your role doesn't particularly need God's empowering. However, in this passage from Acts 6 those who were to care for the needy and distribute food would be chosen from those who were 'full of the Spirit and wisdom'. All the ministries of Christ are important for nurturing the wholeness of His presence among us – every role is a holy role – because all we do is for the kingdom of God. I hope this encourages you to see that whatever role you fulfil is dependent on the outflow of God's Spirit-life through you.

> '*Each of you should use whatever gift you have received to serve others, as faithful stewards of God's grace in its various forms*' (**1 Pet. 4:10**).

— **What, if anything, is stopping you from using your spiritual gift?**

> '*Do not think of yourself more highly than you ought, but rather think of yourself with sober judgment, in accordance with the faith God has distributed to each of you*' (**Rom. 12:3**).

Spiritual gifts are rooted in love because they manifest God. When Paul spoke about love in 1 Corinthians 13, it wasn't a break from his teaching on *charismata* in the surrounding chapters – he was emphasising that without love, *charismata* are nothing. There is no place for competition, hierarchy or pride in the spiritual life of God.

— **Is love for others your motivation for experiencing more of God's power, or something else?**

Lord, I acknowledge my need of Your anointing for the work You have asked me to do. Please empower me with those rich blessings and resources of Your Spirit-life that I need. Come, Holy Spirit, be pleased to dwell within me more fully and to flow out to nourish others. I believe You can do immeasurably more than I can ask or imagine. I open my heart in faith, and ask You to fill me to full measure with Yourself. Amen.

Restoring the outflow —
through spiritual battle

'take your stand… stand your ground… stand firm then' (**Eph. 6:10–14**)

Lord, I believe I have authority over the spiritual enemy, but my belief isn't often apparent in my day-to-day life. Help me engage with the power of Your Spirit to counter the enemy's influence on myself and on other people. Amen.

Soon after giving my life to Jesus, I started hearing about how we are called to 'fight the good fight of faith' (1 Tim. 6:12) and found myself reading books on the nature of spiritual battle, demonic warfare and territorial spirits. I learnt quite a lot about these subjects in theory, but apart from a quick dabble in prayer here and there, I wasn't really getting involved myself. As a young member of an intercessory group, I'd listen to others taking their prayerful stand against the demonic realm but felt personally inadequate to do the same. I was hesitant because I felt that I was too young, too ungodly, that I lacked sufficient scriptural knowledge, that I still didn't really understand how to pray despite reading all those books and, if I'm honest, feared what would happen if a demon actually manifested while I was praying against it.

That fear wasn't entirely unfounded as there are aspects of the battle (exorcism, for example) in which we oughtn't to participate without mature spiritual discernment and prayerful support. It was quite some time before I appreciated my need to take a stand as a warrior of Christ in every attitude and circumstance, rather than just leaving it to prayer meetings. (You can read more about this in my book, *Prepared for Spiritual Battle*[23].)

There is a scale of perspective regarding spiritual battle. Some people will be at one end, so fixated by the demonic that they've taken their eyes off Jesus and it's become an unhealthy preoccupation potentially filling them with fear. Others will blame everything on demonic activity, and not accept personal responsibility when something is simply their fault. At the other end of the scale, however, are believers who haven't given it much thought; they're disinterested in the subject or remain unconvinced that it impacts their lives in the world to any degree. Wherever we sit along that scale, it is helpful to remember not to take the power and influence of our spiritual enemy lightly, or assume it doesn't affect us, while at the same time maintaining the right perspective and claiming ultimate victory through the death and resurrection of Jesus Christ.

Enemies in the Promised Land

Historically it was the Canaanites, Philistines, Amalekites, Ammonites, Midianites, Babylonians and then the Romans who were hounding or oppressing God's people. Today, our God-given 'promised-land life' has a spiritual enemy biting at its borders; an enemy determined to hold back the outflow of God's Spirit-life from impacting and bearing fruit in the world. God is not stuck in an ongoing battle with the enemy. Satan's hold over spiritual life was defeated through Jesus at the cross, and provided we are in Jesus, the enemy has no hold on us either. But Satan and his dominion of spiritual powers continues to sow lies in the minds of the unsaved, and tries to block the flow of God's power by oppressing His people. Consequently, we still live in enemy territory. Warfare in the spiritual realm is a daily reality for everyone. Although some believers are particularly anointed to exorcise demons, all of us, as Christians, need to stand against worldly principalities and powers to restore the outflow of God's victory against Satan.

'Satan' means adversary, constantly challenging and opposing God's nature and purpose. John 5:19 says: 'the whole world is under the control of the evil one', while one commentary states that Satan is 'the unseen power behind all unbelief and ungodliness'[24]; the god of this age. Satan is pushing and harassing to be master over our lives, and scheming for our attention to choose his ways over God's.

Jesus said, 'In this world you will have trouble' (John 16:33). However, even though we are *in* a world controlled by the enemy, we are no longer *of* this world because our life is 'hidden with Christ' (Col. 3:3). Jesus also said, 'But take heart! I have overcome the world' (John 16:33). We have nothing to fear as we have authority in Christ.

'we have nothing to fear as we have authority in Christ.'

Satan is the father of lies – the deceiver. Lying is his native language, but we know the truth and 'the truth will set [us] free' (John 8:32). He is the tempter; he deceives us with lies then tempts us to respond, but Jesus 'will also provide a way out so that [we] can endure it' (1 Cor. 10:13). He is the accuser; once he has tempted us to sin, he tries to immerse us in overwhelming shame, condemnation and guilt by hurling insults at us such as, 'you're no good, you're a failure', but 'there is now no condemnation for those who are in Christ Jesus' (Rom. 8:1). None! Condemnation is not the same as God's spiritual conviction. God is faithful. If we confess, He will forgive.

Satan is powerful: he can inflict sickness, acts of destruction and even influence the thoughts and actions of people who don't love God, but he is only as powerful as God permits. We should be aware of these powers and not dabble in things like the occult, but take strength from the fact that Christ in us 'is greater than the one who is in the world' (1 John 4:4).

Our enemy will try and gain a foothold in our lives through an unconfessed sin or ungodly habits, which is why we need to 'Be alert and of sober mind. Your enemy the devil prowls around like a roaring lion looking for someone to devour. Resist him, standing firm in the faith' (1 Pet. 5:8–9).

He will also try to build strongholds in our behaviour: persistent cycles of sin that allow the enemy to exploit and inflict damage on ourselves or others. If, for example, we persist in unrighteous anger, it encourages divisive arguments and potential bitter estrangement from others. If we persist in gluttony or drunkenness, it will abuse the gift and nature of God's holy living temple in our lives. If we let Satan build strongholds of fear, doubt, idolatry or impurity within us, let's see these things for what they are – contradiction of God's truth – and reject them in the power of God's righteousness and His Word.

Let's not allow the unbelief of others to undermine our own

faith and experience. The devil is cunning and schemes against us in order to distract, discourage or disillusion us from fulfilling our God-given potential for the kingdom, but in Christ we can take our 'stand against the devil's schemes' (Eph.6:11).

Restoring the outflow of God's Spirit-empowered authority

Set our mind and heart on things above

Many of us live in a 'seeing is believing' culture, which dismisses spiritual activity. This mindset can subtly infiltrate the thinking of anyone whose heart and mind is immersed in the visible realm. Paul, however, reminds us that 'our struggle is not against flesh and blood, but against the rulers, against the authorities, against the powers of this dark world and against the spiritual forces of evil in the heavenly realms' (Eph. 6:12). So let's keep an eye on the reality of the spiritual realm – both the good, and the evil – as we seek to live in harmony with God's Spirit-life in the world.

Worship the King of kings

We need to be aware of Satan and equipped to stand against him, but with our eyes fixed on Jesus. To worship the living Lord is powerful. The enemy hates the name of Jesus on our lips, most especially when He's enthroned in our hearts, minds and wills.

'To worship the living Lord is powerful.'

Wield the sword of the Spirit

The sword of the Spirit is God's Spirit-led use of His Word. We need to continue to get to know it and be empowered by it as we discern God's Spirit-breathed Word for each occasion. The enemy knows how to distort and misuse the Bible, but we can learn from Jesus who would have none of it: 'It is written … It is also written … Away from me, Satan! For it is written…' (Matt. 4:1–11). God's truth sets us free from enemy footholds and strongholds. If we've fallen prey to his lies, letting him undermine our salvation and trust in God, believing the promises and acting on them will transform our thinking, choices and responses. When prompted by the Spirit, let's wield the sword over other people and situations too. Reading, listening and leaning on to God's Word will result in a powerful outflow of His Sovereignty.

Pray in the Spirit

Paul teaches us to pray Spirit-inspired and empowered prayers on *all* occasions, especially when we need to release our God-given authority over the enemy and appropriate Christ's victory. We don't need to be afraid, rather we can stand confidently in who we are in Christ, and who He is in us.

First, we need to allow God to search our hearts and convict us of any sin that we might need to bring before Him, because unconfessed sins gives the enemy a foothold which might hamper the power of our prayers. We can then wait on God for spiritual discernment: a scripture, a word of knowledge, a strategy to pray; humble our hearts to be led instead of dictating to God what we think He should do.

Proactive prayer can mean 'wrestling in prayer' (Col. 4:12). It takes commitment to stay alert and maintain a constant watch; to persevere when emotions are low, when energy dips or we lack motivation. However, our prayer life can strengthen and grow as we pray in the Spirit, and are guided and empowered by the name of Jesus on whom we depend for authority.

Live in the opposite Spirit

Understanding demonic activity isn't complicated or reserved for the 'super-spiritual', it is simply the outworking of evil against God's righteousness; for example, hate opposing love, greed opposing self-control, despair opposing hope and resentment opposing forgiveness. The enemy wants us to grieve the Spirit of God rather than live in the fullness of His empowering. You, me and everyone else will be tempted to choose Satan's ways, and our response to that is as much an act of spiritual warfare as casting out demons: for example, when we're tempted to deceive, we choose to speak the truth; tempted to criticise, we choose to encourage; tempted to be rude, we choose to be kind; tempted to hate, we choose to love; tempted to resent, we choose to forgive; tempted to be greedy, we choose moderation. In short, in every situation seeking to 'keep in step with the Spirit' (Gal. 5:25).

Remember to put on spiritual armour

It is the spiritual armour of God that enables us to stand against the enemy, time and time again. Putting on the armour of God isn't a dressing up exercise, it's a 'remaining in' Jesus, who *is* our armour. Jesus is our protection and empowering, our entire defence and means of attack against the spiritual realm. Apart from Him, we can do nothing. Putting on the armour is to live within His truth and not ignore conviction, to be confident in the message of the gospel and the security of who we are in God. It is to guard against fiery darts of temptation, criticism, condemnation and injustice, which will try to inflame guilt, pride, shame or retaliation. As we dwell in God's Word and wield it with confidence, let's protect our thought patterns from attacks of the enemy. In Jesus, 'we are more than conquerors through him who loved us' (Rom. 8:37).

We have the victory over the enemy for 'the one who is in you is greater than the one in the world' (1 John 4:4), and we can 'be strong in the Lord and in his mighty power' (Eph. 6:10). Even though there is much that might undermine us, we have nothing to fear but everything to fight for on behalf of the unsaved, Christ's Church and our own fruitfulness in 'promised-land life'. I pray that you will be determined to stand firm and release the full potential of God's power for your life.

Getting personal – making this real

'Wrestling is one of the most fatiguing of all competitive sports. The pitting of skill and muscle against one's opponent in such sport is extremely demanding. This is the kind of battle we face with these invisible spiritual beings. The picture is one of close, demanding, fatiguing encounter... How tragic and heartbreaking it is to see believers reeling and staggering under Satan's assault with little hope of victory. The victory is already provided. It remains for us only to aggressively use it and not passively assume it.' Mark I. Bubeck[25]

'For though we live in the world, we do not wage war as the world does. The weapons we fight with are not the weapons of the world. On the contrary, they have divine power to demolish strongholds. We demolish arguments and every pretension that sets itself up against the knowledge of God, and we take captive every thought to make it obedient to Christ' (**2 Cor. 10:3–5**).

— **What has been your perspective of spiritual forces of evil and the battle we face?**

— **Be honest with yourself and with God if you've been fearful, disinterested, or over-confident without relying on God's Spirit-life empowering. How might God be speaking to you to overcome that?**

— **What battlegrounds for prayer do you feel burdened to be part of?**

— **How might wearing the following elements of God's armour affect your focus, confidence, emotional and spiritual wellbeing, and equip you to live and work out your faith?**
  - **The belt of truth**
  - **The breastplate of righteousness**
  - **Feet fitted with the readiness of the gospel of peace**
  - **The shield of faith**
  - **The helmet of salvation**
  - **The sword of the Spirit which is the Word of God**

Lord, I am honoured to be part of Your kingdom army. Restore in me a right perspective on the daily battle I face, and empower me by Your Spirit to stand against the enemy. Help me to apply Your authority, and proclaim victory in Your name. Amen.

Part Four

RESTORING THE BALANCE BEYOND THIS BOOK

To be a 'thin place'

'Surely the LORD is in this place, and I was not aware of it… How awesome is this place! This is none other than the house of God; this is the gate of heaven.' (**Gen. 28:16–17**)

'Thin place' doesn't appear in either my dog-eared or online dictionaries, but this ancient Celtic term describes a place where the presence of God is experienced more readily than others; where the distance between heaven and earth has grown particularly thin so the divine and the secular might more readily meet; or where the Spirit of God is especially present and keenly felt, in ways that transcend our physical senses.

I've often used 'thin place' to describe how I feel whenever I teach at Waverley Abbey House, the home of CWR. It sometimes comes to mind when I sit in a chair overlooking our garden, to spend time in prayer and reading Scripture – days when my connection with the divine feels particularly acute. I'm rather fond of the 'thin place' analogy, but as it doesn't appear in the Bible, I'm careful not to assume its world-view interpretation that God's presence is limited to certain places, especially those that are isolated and quiet – places we might usually visit for a spiritual retreat, or to marvel at God's awesome creation.

Being quiet, alone or inspired by God's brushstrokes of beauty in the great outdoors can be helpful to still busy minds and hearts, discern God's voice and connect with His Spirit more meaningfully than in the humdrum of routine. In fact, Jesus models the importance of withdrawing alone to quiet places to be with our Father undisturbed. But there are many other times and places when we can engage with the heavenly realm. God is found, felt and known in the sharing of His Word in a small group gathering, in the arm around the shoulder of a broken soul, and in the hands and smile reaching out to support and care for the needy. We can sense the presence of God in the volume of a church service with crying toddlers, laughing children, and adults singing praise to the beat of drums and electric guitar; in the bustle of a busy city-centre as we stop to share coffee with a homeless person huddled up in a doorway; in the discomfort of our convicted spirit, which needs to be put right with God's holy ways; in the sadness and frustration of a refugee help-centre; in homes sheltering the violated lives of sex-trafficking victims; or the din of the workforce building an orphanage. We can even sense God's presence in the thick of a traffic jam if we would turn our attention onto God with us. Stillness and solitude may help us discern God's voice, but they aren't the only places where we can sense His presence.

'God is found… in the arm around the shoulder of a broken soul'

Jesus, the perfect 'thin place'

'Thin place' may not be a biblical term, but Adam and Eve walked and talked with God in the Garden of Eden just as God had intended: God living with His people in an intimate, face-to-face relationship. Jacob sensed the presence of God at Bethel, saying: 'This is none other than the house of God; this is the gate of heaven' (Gen. 28:17), and when Solomon built the Jerusalem Temple, the cloud of God's glory filled it with such a great weight of His presence that the priests were unable to fulfil their ministry. However, the most poignant example of God's Spirit-life touching the earth was apparent in the life of Jesus. Immanuel was the dwelling place of the fullness of God, living as a man among His people. In Jesus, there was no barrier between heaven and earth. He was the perfect bridge between life in the unseen heavenly realm and life in the physical world by being both God and man. He manifested the reality of the heavenly realm through divine grace, wisdom and supernatural miracles teaching that it is the openness of our hearts, minds and souls that will enable us to encounter His Spirit, rather than being in a particular physical place.

Jesus was God, but He was also fully human, and the disciplines of His flesh enabled this perfect, infallible bridge. Nothing was more important to Him than being right with his Father, and the fullness of God's Spirit inhabiting and revealing Himself in Jesus' earthly body. Jesus wasn't just a 'thin place' between the spiritual and physical, Jesus brought heaven right into the realm of the world. Thanks to Jesus, we can now experience the Spirit-life of God for ourselves.

'Jesus brought heaven right into the realm of the world.'

The day will come when the distance between heaven and earth, between man and God, will cease – but for now, we can learn from Jesus who epitomised the nature of a 'thin place'. He was the person in whom His followers experienced God's presence. Together we are Christ's Church and God meets with His gathered people, but we are also a dispersed Church called to permeate the world with His presence. We will never know the perfect fullness of Spirit like Jesus does, but the Eden experience of walking with God in both rest and in work, the meeting of the heavenly and earthly realm at Bethel, and the Temple encounter of the all-consuming proximity of God's presence are examples in the Bible of the balance between God's Spirit-life with physical lives that we can seek to experience in greater measure today.

We have supernatural, spiritual resources to shape, guide and empower our natural life and to enrich the lives of others. We are, in effect, the gateway of heaven for others to experience God's goodness as we nurture the inflow and outflow of His Spirit-life in and through us. We live in Christ and His Spirit lives in us. If we long to restore a healthier balance between our physical and spiritual lives then we can practise *being* a 'thin place': connecting His heavenly presence to the families, work places, and other parts of life that we each inhabit.

Getting personal – making this real

'There was no false divide between the sacred and secular.
Where an integrated life, of body and soul, work and worship,
wonder and ordinariness; prayer and life are the norm.
A sacramental outlook that because it sees God in everything,
encourages a reverence for God's creation and a respect for the
care of his world. An everyday spirituality of ordinariness
accessible to all. Never anti–intellectual it was an earthed

*spirituality that met people where they were. People did not
have to climb ecclesiastical walls or learn "holy God speak"
to encounter "a thin place".'* Trevor Miller[26]

— **Has your life in the world felt out of balance with your
life in Christ because a deep hurt has left you
struggling to forgive someone?**

You might not always feel able to forgive, but restoring the balance
is about being the gateway to heaven's forgiveness. It may take
time or require help from a counsellor, but if you are struggling
to forgive someone, bring to mind the nature of your life as a
'thin place' between heaven and earth – a gateway to the one
from whom you've already received mercy – so that you might be
able to pass mercy on to others. Forgiveness may not bring about
justice, but it will bring about healing and release to resume a life
flowing freely and fully in Christ.

— **Do you need to open your heart to the Holy Spirit, to
help you forgive someone today?**

You're not expected to cope alone. Restoring the balance is about
heaven's rest, flowing through your life imbuing calm, clarity and
assurance, even within that busyness. Open your heart to God's
Spirit right now.

— **Has your life in the world felt out of balance with your
life in Christ because of busyness or stress?**

— **Has your life in the world felt out of balance with your life in Christ because you're unsure of the way forward, of which path to take, or confused by so many opinions and possibilities?**

You're not expected to make major decisions alone. Restoring the balance is about God filling you with the knowledge of His will through all spiritual wisdom and understanding. If you need guidance from God, ask Him, and believe with thanks that He *will* provide it.

— **Has your life in the world felt out of balance with your life in Christ because you find it hard to say 'no' to requests from family, friends, colleagues or your church, which puts more pressure on your limited time than God intends for you?**

You are not responsible for everyone and everything; even Jesus didn't agree to do everything that the disciples urged Him to do in response to the demanding crowds. Restoring the balance includes being able to decline a request that doesn't clearly line up with God's purpose for you. Sometimes it is helpful to resist the pressure to reply to a request immediately, and instead say that you will pray for guidance. This releases you from their immediate expectations of you.

— **What request have you received that you need to pray about before responding?**

Lord, Your life paints a beautiful and inspiring picture of the place where heaven met earth through the harmony of God's Spirit living in man. Lord, may this become an increasing reality in my life too, that I may be one of Your gateways to the world. Amen.

Nurturing the 'thin place'

'The coming of the kingdom of God is not something that can be observed, nor will people say, "Here it is," or "There it is," because the kingdom of God is in your midst.' (**Luke 17:20–21**)

Lord, I do believe that the heavenly realm is already part of my life through Your indwelling Spirit, but so often the world overshadows this awesome truth. Please help me to hone a Christlike harmony between the two. Amen.

Mum and I hadn't been more than ten minutes in Worcester Cathedral, when we entered the Jesus Chapel and the weight of God's presence seemed almost tangible. Surely this epitomised a 'thin place'?

I held back momentarily, trying to put into words what I was sensing in my soul. Perhaps it was the thick stone walls, muffling the outside world. Perhaps it was the high-vaulted ceilings, imbuing a sense of spaciousness. Or had centuries of praise and prayer right there on that spot, weakened the 'walls' between the world and the spiritual realm? I couldn't say for sure, but just as a cathedral's 'thin place' ambience focuses attention on God, so we can nurture a 'thin place' in our own lives by growing more attentive to His presence, whatever we are doing or whoever we are with.

In previous chapters we've looked at stilling our thoughts and emotions, of being present with God and for people, of being God's safe and spacious place to needy individuals, and of being His living temple. Now we will bring all these themes together as one as we focus on, in increasing measure, the balance between God's Spirit-life and our life in the world.

Worcester Cathedral sits on a busy junction in the city centre. The audible noise of general traffic, pedestrian crossings and raucous students combine with the 'silent' noise of the lure of a large shopping centre, the pressure of earning a liveable wage, and the culture of cynicism and unbelief; distractions that potentially suffocate spiritual life with their urban fumes. Fortunately, the cathedral boasts a dense, stone-walled boundary, stifling the noise and putting the world on mute, raising spiritual antennae to God's presence.

'We can learn to still the interference and obtain an inner core of stillness in God'

We don't have to visit a cathedral to still the noise of the world: its demanding voices, opinions and expectations; its blaming, shaming, mocking and rebutting; and its gods of materialism, ego, image and success. We can learn to still the interference and obtain an inner core of stillness in God and an ear fine-tuned to His Spirit, not just when we're alone in prayer, but while out and about in the day.

Psalm 46:10 says: 'Be still, and know that I am God'. Stilling our racing hearts and minds, even for just a few moments, reminds us to intentionally focus on God with us. It reconnects our awareness of our lives in Christ and the Spirit-life truth that the kingdom of God is within, and we can take that stillness – that deepening awareness and intimacy – back into the task at hand.

The lofty airiness of a cathedral inspires one to be fully present, to take stock of the vast spaciousness of a place filled for centuries with praise and prayer, and to sense God's presence in response. If pressed for time or distracted with chatter, the awe and inspiration may be lost on us, but being fully present to engage with its grandeur inspires reverence for the God it honours, creativity from its beauty, and encouragement to take that breathing space of God back out to the world.

David wrote: 'They confronted me in the day of my disaster, but the Lord was my support. He brought me out into a spacious place; he rescued me because he delighted in me' (Psa. 18:18–19). We can think of dwelling in the spacious place as being present in each moment; to observe from God's perspective and discern His response. It is to know this is where we should be right now and that we are a gateway of God for a certain person, task, situation or prayer. It's to know that His grace is sufficient for today; to accept His empowering for the task at hand. It is to feel His love for the shamed and blamed, and His grief for a world that turns its back on Him. It's about focusing on God, listening for His guidance, and honouring Him in the here and now with our words, behaviour, attitudes and responses. It is our spiritual awareness of God inhabiting earth in every moment; in the magnificence of a stunning landscape; in the cry of a newborn; and in the tears of the grieving.

'we are a gateway of God for a certain person, task, situation or prayer.'

Life can sometimes hold us back from the freedom of being present in the spacious place of God's presence. Worrying about tomorrow, glancing over our shoulder at yesterday, or allowing some pressing need to impose itself on the 'now' can all diminish our awareness of God with us, and of walking unhindered in His presence.

Many women are skilled at multi-tasking, but doing several things at once means not being able to give one thing our full focus. It can undermine our relationships if someone gets hurt or misunderstood when we fail to love and listen to them with our full attention. It can hold back the best of our work when a job is riddled with mistakes or fails to fulfil its potential when we try to tackle too many projects. It can steal our peace in a busy day when we juggle too many thoughts and tasks in a poor attempt to get everything done. Trying to do too much can mean we miss out on the fulfilled life of Spirit and flesh living in perfect harmony, and the wholeness of wellbeing that Jesus offers.

God's presence was never confined to the innermost sanctuary of the Jerusalem Temple, and He's not confined to cathedrals today. God is omnipresent but commissioned the Temple as a place of focus for the Israelites; a place where His Spirit would be seen to dwell with His people; a place to praise Him, pray to Him, and learn to live lives that honour Him. It was a gateway for anyone who wanted to know Him to draw close and find acceptance as one of His own. A role that each one of us are now called to fulfil.

Jesus said, 'Anyone who loves me will obey my teaching. My Father will love them, and we will come to them and make our home with them' (John 14:23). I love the word 'home' here as it's infused with rich meaning and imagery. For some, it's a place imprinted with personal taste, of security and wellbeing. It might be the habitat of the heart, of loving and being loved. The ethos of 'home' is also how Jesus perceives our potential as living temples, with lives that nurture 24/7 worship as we live for His honour; living temples infused with God's love, inspiring our kingdom service. This is what Paul realised when he wrote: 'Do you not know that your bodies are temples of the Holy Spirit, who is in you, whom you have received from God? You are not your own; you were bought at a price. Therefore honour God with your bodies' (1 Cor. 6:19–20).

To be a 'thin place' is not just about quiet, stillness and rest, but of living with the awareness of God in every part of our lives, so we can then take our stillness in Him, our security in Him, our love for and being loved by Him out into our day. That's when the fullness of God's Spirit-life in us reaches out to draw others to Him.

Our spirituality isn't reserved for when we're at church, reading the Bible or praying. Our spirituality is part of our physicality and should influence every part of life, be it parenting, caring for dependants, volunteering, secular or Christian employment. Whatever our 24/7 routine, we can *all* be the gateway to God for the saved and unsaved. The more we restore the balance of being open to God's Spirit-life instead of filling ourselves with the world's paraphernalia, the greater kingdom impact and influence we'll have.

'Our spirituality is part of our physicality and should influence every part of life'

God was exceptionally present where Jesus was present, and God wants to use us to be supernaturally present that all may experience His love and grace through the presence of His people, wherever they are.

Getting personal – making this real

> *'The most holy practice, the nearest to daily life, and the most essential for the spiritual life, is the practice of the presence of God, that is to find joy in his divine company and to make it a habit of life, speaking humbly and conversing lovingly with him at all times, every moment, without rule or restriction, above all at times of temptation, distress, dryness, and revulsion, and even of faithlessness and sin.'*
> Brother Lawrence[27]

— **Be still, and know God with you…**

- Remind yourself to take moments to be still during your day: a pause to look out the window, to shift your attention away from your screen, to close your eyes momentarily while waiting in a queue, and let the eyes of your heart fix their attention on Jesus.

- Know and engage with His presence with you – His love enfolding, His peace imbuing, His power enabling, His wisdom clarifying, His comfort embracing, His strength re-energising, and His grace reshaping your natural reactions in line with a kingdom response. 'Jesus is with me; the kingdom of God is within me; God's Spirit-life is within me.' Turn up the volume of this truth in your heart until it drowns out the clamouring noise occupying your world.

- 'My heart is not proud, LORD, my eyes are not haughty; I do not concern myself with great matters or things too wonderful for me. But I have calmed and quieted myself, like a weaned child with its mother; like a weaned child I am content' (Psa. 131:1–2). Reflect on the implication of this psalm. A weaned child feels the closeness of its mother and is content in her love, trusting her to provide food as needed, secure in her protection, guided by her wisdom and learning from her as their primary role-model. See your soul as that child with Jesus. How does this image encourage you to dwell unhindered and unperturbed in His presence?
- Being mindful of the goodness of God with you is something you can do at any time in the day to slow down your thoughts and rest your soul; to shift your focus away from the demands, fears, or distractions, and focus on God with you.

— **Live and walk unhindered in God's spacious place…**
   If you're struggling to be present in the place of God's calling right 'now', pause for a moment to let go and give thanks.
- Let go of the past that still troubles you – that awkward meeting this morning, the uncompleted task, or the delayed health result.
- Let go of guilt or animosity by asking God to prompt what you may need to put right in your heart, praying for any people involved, and by handing over situations into His loving care until it's time to resume the conversation or undertaking.
- Let go of any of tomorrow's deadlines that are trying to steal your attention from today. Root yourself in God's love to

guard against fears gnawing at your heart and distracting your sense of God with you right now in the task at hand.

- Give thanks for the good memories of yesterday, the hopes for tomorrow and for God's gift of His being with you today.

- Now open the spiritual eyes of your heart to see Him, and to marvel at His majestic splendour and infinite love; to discern His heart for the person you're with; to ask for His wisdom for the situation you face; and to empower and equip you for the task He has called you to do in this moment. Then walk unhindered by distraction, fear or anxiety, and be free to serve in the outflow of His Spirit-life anointing you in the spacious place of His presence.

— **Honour the living temple that is your life!**
- Today is the day, like every day, to build, maintain and honour God in His temple of your life. Do you feel 'at home' with God, His love, His character and His priorities? If not, what stops you feeling that way, and how can you put that right?

- You are the house of God. What materials are you building it with? Reflect on how your life, ambitions, attitudes, words and behaviour reflect God's love, ways and will. How 'at home' is the Spirit of God in you?

- Picture the relationships, tasks, hobbies and commitments that fill your week. How might you act differently if you saw yourself as God's living temple, honouring Him in all you say and do, and *always* living out of that place of love?

- How might you act differently if you saw yourself as a 'thin place': a gateway for others to meet with God in you?

Lord, I do believe Your kingdom is within me, the presence of Your Spirit-life infusing my very soul. May this gateway to Your Spirit-life always remain open to everyone I meet or communicate with today. Amen.

Taking possession of 'promised-land life'

'As I was with Moses, so I will be with you; I will never leave you nor forsake you. Be strong and courageous, because you will lead these people to inherit the land I swore to their ancestors to give them… Be strong and courageous. Do not be afraid; do not be discouraged, for the LORD your God will be with you wherever you go.' (Josh. 1:5–6,9)

Lord, I do believe You are completely dependable and trustworthy. Please help me overcome the things that hold me back from putting my belief into practice. Amen.

Confidence doesn't come naturally to me but God has been taking me on a journey of growing my confidence in Him, and helping me to take hold of His 'promised-land life'.

As a child I was painfully shy: clinging to my mother's skirts instead of taking my place at the barre in ballet school, turning down an opportunity to join the oversubscribed Brownies, and afraid to return to class after break unless I was with a close friend. Even as I matured, I avoided large groups because I was too timid to speak up – and I still struggle to join a huddle of people who are chatting over coffee after church. I was constantly afraid of making mistakes, a people-pleaser to the hilt and more willing to be used (and for a period, abused) than to stand up for who I was or what I believed. I am still 'naturally' shy, but God has restored my confidence in Him – 'supernatural' confidence – to let Him use me as a public speaker.

My early years of faith were so knocked by significant others who regarded me as ignorant, foolish or brainwashed that fear stopped me sharing my beliefs with people. However, God has nurtured such confidence in Him, and in who He is, that I'm no longer ashamed about the Jesus I know and believe. When my brother battled alcoholism, attempted suicide and then died at 43 years old, my journey with God gave me confidence that prayer is still powerful. And when an onslaught of uncustomary health problems propelled my name to the top of emergency lists, God gently increased my confidence in Him as my ultimate help and hope.

In whom, or what, are you placing your confidence?

If you've got to this chapter without jumping ahead then you've almost finished the book, and hopefully on your way to restoring the balance of God's Spirit-life impacting your life in the world. However, as I said earlier, the balance will always depend on the degree to which you are willing to put your belief in God into practice, so much so that if God isn't in control, you may fall flat. That kind of living is going to need confidence, not in yourself or in anyone else but in God.

Confidence may be a strong feeling of trust in a person or thing, or a belief in our own ability. But even confidence in

God can be undermined in so many ways: by atheism with its convincing arguments that suggest we've been misled in believing biblical truth; by prayers that remain unanswered despite the promise we will receive whatever we ask; by the pain of unresolved problems that seem to mock the suggestion that God cares for us; and by a world seemingly out of control, frightening and, at times, threatening despite so many scriptures proclaiming the sovereignty of God.

Confidence in God is also undermined by substitute places of perceived security, such as: our confidence in our skills and abilities; in the company, advice and help of a spouse or special friend; in a savings account, pension plan or financial investment; in employment or in being needed by others; in adopting certain behaviour patterns; or opting to wear a mask to disguise the real 'me'. Just a few of the many alternatives to confidence in God that appear to promise present or future security, even though they could suddenly let us down and undermine our peace and wellbeing.

Confidence in God, however, is being at ease with who we are in God, and assured of who God is in us. It is the inflow of His comfort, guidance, empowering and wholeness of wellbeing that sustains the outflow of kingdom life even when we're facing fear or difficulty. It is the innate trust in His character, promises and power that keeps us composed and at peace, with a sense of security that inspires us to live with boldness and courage.

'Confidence in God… is being at ease with who we are… and assured of who God is in us.'

Both the world and our spiritual enemy will try to lure our source of confidence away from God, but Jeremiah 17 encourages us to restore our confidence in God and to take hold of 'promised-land life':

> *'Cursed is the one who trusts in man, who draws strength from mere flesh and whose heart turns away from the LORD. That person will be like a bush in the wastelands; they will not see prosperity when it comes. They will dwell in the parched places of the desert, in a salt land where no one lives. But blessed is the one who trusts in the LORD, whose confidence is in him. They will be like a tree planted by the water that sends out its roots by the stream. It does not fear when heat comes; its leaves are always green. It has no worries in a year of drought and never fails to bear fruit.'* (**Jer. 17:5–8**)

Restoring the balance of confidence in God

To restore the balance – to experience the promised fullness of God's Spirit-life infusing our life in the world – is not a life to be earned or assumed, but a life to be taken hold of. The Israelites took possession of the Promised Land by trusting God, devoting themselves to Him and honouring Him. We need to do the same.

Jeremiah 17:5–8 is one of my personal go-to scriptures during intensive phases of work when I'm fighting for time and energy to juggle writing deadlines, speaking engagements, family, home life and church responsibilities. It was during one such period that I scribbled down the following in my journal, based on Jeremiah's picture:

Worried, fretful, weak, uninspired, fruitless, stressed is Anne when she trusts in herself and her own capabilities to enable her. But blessed – at peace, content, assured and enriched – is Anne when she trusts God for equipping, and puts her confidence in His capability and anointing. The heat has come! A very intense schedule [I named each task], but Anne has nothing to fear if her roots are deep in God's life-giving water.

When I trusted in myself to cope and complete everything on time, my stress levels soared and my health began to suffer; my life looked more like a wasteland than an enriched and fruitful land. But when I trusted in God to enable me to cope and complete those tasks, it infused my life with peace, expectation and assurance. The key was knowing whether or not I felt God had called me to do all those things on that list, and because I did, I could put my confidence in Him to enable me to fulfil them.

To be blessed by God is to experience the inflow of His Spirit-life imparting contentment, fulfilment, satisfaction, enrichment and peace. These spiritual blessings replace the unstable emotions of doubt, defeat, disillusionment, frustration and gloom. So to be blessed is not about the nature of our circumstances; spiritual blessings are our Father's gift in the good times *and* in the struggles and storms of life. This perspective helps us trust in the Lord and believe deep in our soul that God works for the good of those who love Him, even in the fallout of this imperfect world, and that He is

'spiritual blessings are our Father's gift in the good times *and* in the struggles and storms of life.'

for us and not against us. We are then able to put our confidence in Him; to rely on Him for assurance, identity and poise, for a sense of wellbeing and meaning to life, for strength, resilience and enabling. When we do that, we become like the tree that sends out its roots by the stream.

Roots take up life-essential water, but they also anchor a tree, giving it strength and resilience even in the fiercest storms or 'when the heat comes' (Jer. 17:8). Heat and drought symbolise the difficulties, oppression and impoverishment we can face. Fear, uncertainty or grief are just some of the distractions that can tear our focus away from our life in Christ, as we seek 'abundant life' from other sources. But if we choose to remain in Jesus – in ways that have been explained in Part Two – our roots in Him will keep us strong and we will be able to bear fruit. When we put our confidence in God it encourages, releases and enables us to be fruitful for God's kingdom whatever situation we face, however inadequate we feel, or whatever 'natural' feelings would try to hold us back.

It is helpful to clarify here that the meaning of 'cursed' in verse five has nothing to do with demonic possession. It describes a place that isn't experiencing a fulfilled and fruitful life. When we trust in ourselves, or fail to trust in who God made us to be, or when we place our trust in someone or something other than God (eg money, appearance, ability), our spiritual lives begin to look like a wasteland or desert: lacking growth, productivity, and meaningful kingdom influence.

Putting our trust in ourselves can foster a brash, arrogant confidence driven by competitiveness and serving our ego; a me-first, 'I can do anything I want' self-confidence that we sometimes fall prey to in the world, but which is fruitless for God's kingdom. Conversely, it can also foster a sense of insecurity and inadequacy, a fear of failure or a low self-esteem, and hold us back from fulfilling our God-given potential.

By putting our confidence in God, however, we can be at ease with who God made us to be with no need to compare or compete with others. We can be secure enough to take risks and make mistakes. With God, we are assured that this harmony between our physical and spiritual lives – the empowering inflow of God's Spirit-life – *will* bear kingdom fruit.

Getting personal – making this real

'Christians are called believers, but many times, we are more like unbelieving believers. We trust our friends, the bank, the stock market or the government more than we trust God and His Word.' Joyce Meyer[28]

Putting your confidence in God is essential for taking possession of 'promised-land life': restoring the balance between God's Spirit-life and your life in the world.

— **How would you feel if you were able to put your confidence in God for some aspect of your life? Would you act differently?**

— **How do Jeremiah's words inspire you to restore your confidence in God?**

— **Who or what have you put your security in?**

— How does putting your confidence in things other than God undermine your gifts, worth and purpose as God's child?

— What does Scripture say about God's character and promises? Does it give you confidence?

Lord, I am challenged that I don't rely on You as I should, and that I'm holding back a part of my life from the fullness of all You want to do in and through me. Help me restore my confidence in You, and to anticipate a 'promised-land life' filled with the fullness of Your love and empowering. Amen.

Restoring the balance beyond this book

'a woman called Martha opened her home to him. She had a sister called Mary, who sat at the Lord's feet listening to what he said. But Martha was distracted by all the preparations that had to be made. She came to him and asked, "Lord, don't you care that my sister has left me to do the work by myself? Tell her to help me!"
"Martha, Martha," the Lord answered, "you are worried and upset about many things, but few things are needed – or indeed only one. Mary has chosen what is better, and it will not be taken away from her.' (**Luke 10:38–42**)

In the film *A Good Year*[29], Max (played by Russell Crowe) is a successful, cut-throat trader in London's stock exchange. He learns that he has inherited his uncle's home and vineyard in France; a home of fond memories and deep impressions from childhood visits. Money-focused Max has long since lost touch with his kindly uncle, so thinks nothing of selling the property to make an immediate gain. But there is a problem. In order to sell, he will have to visit France to sign the documents.

'Why are you selling?' someone asks him, after he's had time to reacquaint himself with his inheritance.

'This place doesn't suit my life,' he replies.

'No Max, *your* life doesn't suit *this* place.'

The laid-back ambience of a life he had cherished as a boy, the ethos of 'a man's word is his honour', and the seasonal flow of the working land didn't appear to suit the materialistic city life and self-centred decisions that Max had grown accustomed to; they didn't fit with the identity of his demanding, but financially successful, career. His visit to the French chateau, however, fast turns into a life-changing shift of perspective and priorities as it dawns on Max just how much he will miss out on in life, if he chooses his London life over his inheritance.

What about us? Are we living a life that fits with our spiritual inheritance? Restoring the balance can help us evaluate whether we are like Max; whether the life we've been living in the world is at odds with the Spirit-life of God. We might be followers of Jesus, but if we're living in 'Martha mode', we risk missing out on the fullness of our inheritance because we are distracted or dissuaded from the implications of God's presence with us. Instead, let's recognise the choice that needs to be made, each day, for the rest of our life – to choose, like Mary, to be in Jesus' presence. For as A.W. Tozer writes, 'the desire to be filled must be all-consuming. It must be for the time the biggest thing in life, so acute, so intrusive as to crowd out everything else. The degree of fullness in any life accords perfectly with the intensity of true desire. We have as much of God as we actually want.'[30]

Choosing what is better

For many years, my journal was dominated by a question repeatedly scrawled in large red letters: *God, how can I fit it all in?* There were scribbled pictures of stickmen being pulled in too many directions by the demands on my life. There were charts and spider-diagrams attempting to work out how to balance my time appropriately between spiritual needs, like prayer and reading the Bible, and the commitments of my physical life. I even devised a complex computer spreadsheet – and in case you're wondering, no, it was of no help whatsoever!

Deep down, I knew it wasn't right to differentiate between my spiritual and physical life, but that's how it felt in the reality of everyday routine. It seemed that my life had to be like either Martha or Mary, but never both at the same time, and without any hope of striking a balance between the two.

Martha opened her home and heart to Jesus, but she was still preoccupied with life's demands more than she was by His presence. Mary, however, chose to sit at His feet. She chose to be close.

Likewise, some of us are activists by nature, some are contemplatives, while others fall somewhere in between. Neither is wrong in Jesus' eyes, in fact He needs both; we are called to be workers for God's kingdom as well as people who pray. Jesus didn't condemn Martha as the work still needed to be done, but He did honour the better choice Mary had made to prioritise God's Spirit-life, which would last for eternity, unlike the changing and temporary demands of life in the world. The wisdom that was imparted to her from being with Jesus remained with her when she resumed her day. She began to enjoy her spiritual inheritance while still being very much part of this world.

We have an awesome promise of life to the full: our inheritance of God's Spirit-life impacting our natural life in overflowing abundance. Without Jesus we can do nothing of meaningful influence for God's kingdom, but *with* Him, we can do 'immeasurably more than all we can ask or imagine' (Eph. 3:20). Jesus truly is our awesome inheritance for today as well as for eternity.

'We have an awesome promise of life to the full'

I've learnt, and am still learning, that it's too easy to be torn between my physical and spiritual life; between the tangible visible world and God's Spirit-life in me. More importantly, I'm learning that Jesus wants to infiltrate every season and juncture of life. Every decision and path chosen. Every chuckle and every tear. Every fist pump and every failure. Every moment alone or with others. Every embrace and every rejection. Every provision and every need. You can learn that too because *you* are chosen. You are not at the end of the queue back at school, longing to be picked for a sports team. You are not stuck in your bedroom, unwelcome or not good enough to be part of the fun downstairs. You are not hidden in the wings at that audition for the amateur dramatics society. You are chosen to be a blessing and influence for God's kingdom.

So I encourage you to root yourself in Gods' love, to know that He delights in you, and to anchor your perspective about who you are in Christ. I pray that you will believe and engage with the awesome truth that God is the source and flow of *all* of your life, and that you will live and move and have your being in

Him. As you step out onto the path He calls you to walk, know that God is for you, that He values what you bring, that He will never abandon you, and that His presence goes with you *always*.

Getting personal – making this real

> *'Is there something more important in our lives than Jesus?*
> *If so, perhaps we will need to make an adjustment. When*
> *Christ becomes not only our life but the thing we live for, we*
> *discover the reality of what he came to bring: not merely*
> *life, but abundant life (John 10:10). Jesus truly is our life.'*
> James Bryan Smith [31]

— **Thinking about your life now, would you say that you live out what you believe?**

— **Is your belief in Jesus evident by what you treasure most deeply in your heart, by the focus of your thoughts, or by how you use your time, resources and gifts?**

— **What new things do you want to put into practice, and what do you want to let go of, to live in greater harmony with God's Spirit-life in you?**

— **How can you restore the balance between being a Martha and being a Mary, and so experience in greater measure, Christ's promise of life to the full?**

Lord, open the eyes of my heart and understanding to help me grasp the glorious life that I can live in You, the awesome riches of my kingdom inheritance, and the incomparably great power available through the Spirit-life of God, working in and out of my life today. Amen.

Endnotes

[1] Oswald Chambers, *My Utmost for His Highest* (London: Marshall, Morgan & Scott, 1927) p123

[2] Francis Foulkes, *Tyndale New Testament Commentaries – Ephesians* (Leicester: IVP, 1989) p54

[3] Commentary in *The Compact NIV Study Bible* (London: Hodder & Stoughton, 1987) p1781

[4] Canon J.John, @Canonjjohn Twitter post, 15 May 2018

[5] Richard Holloway, *Paradoxes of Christian Faith and Life* (Oxford: A.R. Mowbray, 1984) p25

[6] W. Phillip Keller, *A Shepherd Looks At Psalm 23* (Grand Rapids, MI, USA: Zondervan, 2007) p59

[7] Selwyn Hughes, *Every Day With Jesus – A Higher Love* (Farnham: CWR, 2018) 18 April

[8] Chris Webb, *God Soaked Life* (London: Hodder & Stoughton, 2017) p97

[9] Philip Yancey, *Prayer* (London: Hodder & Stoughton, 2006) p230

[10] Commentary in *The Compact NIV Study Bible* (London: Hodder & Stoughton, 1987) p1467

[11] Martin L. Smith, *The Word Is Very Near You* (Plymouth: Cowley Publications, 1989) p20

[12] Rev Stephen Charnock, *The Works of the late Rev. Stephen Charnock* (London: Baynes, 1815) p310 Also *Discourses Upon the Existence and Attributes of God, Volume 1* (London: T. Tegg, 1840) p135

[13] James Bryan Smith, *Hidden In Christ* (London: Hodder & Stoughton, 2015) p151

[14] Anne Le Tissier, *The Mirror That Speaks Back; Looking at, listening to and reflecting your worth in Jesus* (Abingdon: The Bible Reading Fellowship, 2018) p56

[15] Kerri Weems, *Rhythms of Grace: Discovering God's Tempo for Your Life* (Grand Rapids, MI, USA: Zondervan, 2014) p45

[16] Sheridan Voysey, *Open House* (Sydney, Australia: Strand, 2008) p88

[17] Mike Pilavachi, 'Everyday Supernatural', *Premier Christianity*, November 2016, p42

[18] Oswald Chambers, *My Utmost for His Highest* (London: Marshall, Morgan & Scott, 1927) p136

[19] Beauty from Ashes is a charity offering support and encouragement to people whose lives have been distorted or broken through loss and trauma towards faith in, and dependence on, Christ. For further information, visit beautyfromashes.co.uk

[20] Stuart Briscoe, *Spirit Life* (Eastbourne: Kingsway Publications, 1983) p33

[21] Rick Warren, *The Purpose Driven Life* (Grand Rapids, MI, USA: Zondervan, 2002) pp281,284,295

[22] A.W. Tozer, *Keys to the Deeper Life* (Grand Rapids, MI, USA: Zondervan, 1988) p50

[23] Anne Le Tissier, *Prepared for Spiritual Battle* (Farnham: CWR, 2008) pp10–11

[24] Commentary in *The Compact NIV Study Bible* (London: Hodder & Stoughton, 1987) p1733

[25]Mark I. Bubeck, *The Adversary* (Chicago, IL, USA: The Moody Bible Institute, 1975) pp71,77

[26]Trevor Miller, 'Celtic Spirituality – A Beginners Guide' taken from northumbriacommunity.org [Accessed 15 September 2018]

[27]Brother Lawrence, *The Practice of the Presence of God* (London: Hodder & Stoughton, 1981) p68

[28]Joyce Meyer, 'How the Habit of Trust Transforms Your Life' taken from joycemeyer.com [Accessed 20 September 2018]

[29]*A Good Year*, Twentieth Century Fox, 2006

[30]A.W. Tozer, *God's Pursuit of Man* (Chicago, IL, USA: Moody Publishing, 2015)

[31]James Bryan Smith, *Hidden in Christ* (London: Hodder & Stoughton, 2015) p52

Inspiring
Women

CWR's women's ministry, Inspiring Women, exists to help women find their identity in Christ, to give them the keys to gain greater security, significance and self-worth, and access their God-given gifts. There are daily Bible reading notes, books and resources, as well as courses and seminars.

Other books for you...

Unshakeable Confidence

Confidence can take many guises, but what does true, unshakeable confidence look like? Drawing on her own experiences, Jen Baker shares how the truth and strength of God's Word enabled her to journey from debilitating fear to unshakeable confidence. This book will remind you of the power of God's unwavering love, and empower you to become the woman God created you to be.
ISBN: 978-1-78259-840-4

The Beauty Within

How we see ourselves can affect how we feel, behave and experience life. But how does God see us? In the form of a spiritual journey, Rosalyn Derges helps us to realise that God sees us as His daughters, and wants us to grow and develop to reflect His image. This is a beautiful hardback interactive journal with space for you to write, draw and focus on God's truth about the beauty within.
ISBN: 978-1-78259-832-9

Inspiring Women Every Day

Written by women for women, these daily Bible reading notes offer insights that can be applied to your life every day. Discover more titles in the Inspiring Women range on our website.

Courses and Seminars

Our courses and seminars are designed for women of all ages and walks of life, creating opportunities to dig deeper into a relationship with God. Come and enjoy insightful teaching, worship and warm fellowship.

We can also bring some of our courses to your church or small group.

Find out more about all our resources and courses for women at
cwr.org.uk/inspiringwomen